About the Authors

Offering Student Perspective:

Former student of David Fairchild: Elyse Kunzler is an award-winning co-author for *Steering Classes off Cliffs: 10 Ways Professors Sabotage Students to Crash and Burn—Campus Nightmares (Vol. 2)*. She grew up in a small town in Southern Utah and had a desire to write books from the age of four after watching her older brother make her little comic books to read. She received her associates degree from Utah Valley University and her Bachelors degree in English from Brigham Young University. She likes singing loudly (and badly) in her car, playing the piano (mediocrely) and spending time with her nieces and nephews.

Offering Professor Perspective:

David Fairchild has taught university composition for 15 years. He remains a lifelong-learner and is a firm believer in empowering students to discover their control over their own educational tenure. He has had the privilege of working with many of these wonderful people, including Elyse Kunzler. He has worked extensively in amusement and entertainment and is the author of the award winning books *Boom, The Exodus,* and *Steering Classes off Cliffs: 10 Ways Professors Sabotage Students to Crash and Burn—Campus Nightmares (Vol. 2)*.

Jello Freeways:
10 Ways Students Sabotage Their Efforts

Elyse
Kunzler
  and
David
Fairchild

Campus Nightmares (Vol. 1)

A companion to *Steering Classes off Cliffs: 10 Ways Professors Sabotage Their Students to Brash and Burn Campus Nightmares (Vol. 2)*

▋▋▋▋
Four Doors
Publishing

Four Doors Publishing LLC
Spanish Fork, UT

Printed in the United States of America.

A Preface
from the Student

Okay, from someone who has very recently been a student and still in many senses considers herself one, let me just say that I'm sure you're probably sick of hearing from professors.

Am I right?

You hear from them day in and day out—from your classes, to your advisers, even to your club activities. You probably don't want to just read another book where you're going to be lectured by yet another professor, right? Trust me. I've been there. However, I want to take this little moment to vouch for Professor Fairchild and why I agreed to do this book with him, and I think you'll realize that this book isn't just another lecture telling you all the things you're doing wrong in school, but instead a roadmap built from the perspective of both a professor and a student (just like you!) who truly want to help.

Let's do a flashback, shall we? It was my first full semester of college. I had taken some college classes in high school, but this was my first semester as a full-time student, so I was so flipping scared. I had my sister-in-law walk me around campus and show me where all my classes were. I had all of my color-coded binders ready to go, and I had a handy-dandy, new laptop ready for me to take notes with. I was so ready! At least until reality body-slammed into me that first day with the weight of a freight train. And why was that? Because my very first class of the semester was at 8:00 a.m. in a crumbling, musty basement, and it was Professor Fairchild's.

To set the tone even more, there were only about 20 students in the classroom, most of us just out of high school and freshmen who all looked incredibly nervous to be there. We made polite small talk as we waited for the professor, but, as the clock ticked by, no professor came through the door. Just as we started to get nervous and fidgety, the most outspoken of the students, making small talk, stood up, walked over to the podium, and introduced himself as Professor Fairchild. Just like that, all the chittering in the classroom fell into instant silence as each student tried to wrack their brains to see if

i

they had said anything rude or dismissive about Professor Fairchild or his class before he had revealed himself. He didn't even let us catch our breath before he launched into his syllabus, expectations for the class, and the plan for the course.

At the end of that first day, I knew I was in deep water. Although Professor Fairchild's course, assignments and grading seemed like a challenge, it wasn't any of these that instilled fear and anticipation about his class in me. It was the high expectations. I could tell from the get-go how much responsibility would be placed on me—and that scared me—but it also made me really excited. I had never wanted to succeed more in a class than this one, because it seemed like a real challenge. Not only would Professor Fairchild be grading me, but I would be grading myself.

When I say *grading myself*, I don't mean like a letter grade, but rather Professor Fairchild's whole class was set up in such a way that if you failed you really had no one to blame but yourself. He was clear and concise about his expectations and about the consequences if you didn't fulfill those. It didn't seem like there were any safety nets or handrails in this classroom. You failed or succeeded by your own merit with no takebacks. Although the class was intimidating, we had no dropouts that entire semester. It seems like I and the rest of the class welcomed the challenge and wanted to push ourselves.

The reason why all of the students stayed in his class is the same reason I agreed to write these books with my old professor. He genuinely wanted to see each and every single one of us succeed, but he wanted us to get there on our own merits, and that's how he set up his classroom. Everything I learned in that English 2010 class set me up for success in life. He taught me how to defend my beliefs by teaching me how to write a compelling argumentative article on a controversial topic. He taught me about accountability, self-respect and how to deal with people who aren't on your side.

Because of this, Professor Fairchild was the person I trusted to write my letter of recommendation when I transferred to a different university. He genuinely wanted me to succeed and grow wherever I went, even writing the letter for me a year after the completion of the class. He still remembered me and wrote a glowing recommendation that I truly believe that—without it—I wouldn't have been able to go to the school I applied for. Not only that, he helped me with some editing and advice for my own personal fiction project that I've been working on as well.

All of these reasons are why, when Professor Fairchild approached me about this project, I jumped at the opportunity. I can't imagine anyone else as a better candidate for this topic because of his care for students and their successes—not just in the classroom but in life. He has so much experience, stories, and funny anecdotes to tell that I promise will be worthwhile and incredibly helpful. So, as you delve into this book, trust that Professor Fairchild won't be just another Professor talking down to you, but more like a Gandalf the Gray. He'll be a guide and a mentor but he's going to give you the tools to finish the journey on your own and with your own strength. So, without further ado, let's get started!

Fairchild Dedication:

*For K-whyra, Isabel, Haley, Sagar, Carly, Hyrum,
Estrella, Tess, Luke, Devin, Logan, Kamille, Makelle,
Porter, Lili, Riley, Emmalee, Andy, Kyra, Justin
and Brooklyn*

For in case you need proof. . .

*and to remind one of you that it's always been:
"No. I am your father."*

*And to Elyse for agreeing to do this project
and make it possible:*

Thank you.

Table of Contents:

Introduction
from the Professor

What you're about to read are the individual perspectives from a university teacher (Fairchild) and a former student of his (Kunzler) on an array of topics that can interfere with student-learning in the university setting.

To begin, we must start with a word that students of all ages love to use. It's not a swear word, but it might as well be. If teachers earned royalties for every time we heard it, we'd have the highest paid jobs in the world. The word is *effort.*

Effort is commonly accepted to mean a vigorous attempt to accomplish a task.

However, there is another definition—one that students of all ages apply to it.

Student definition of effort: Using the time and energy one has exerted as an excuse to suggest the student has accomplished a task, even though the task has not been accurately completed.

This can offend students when I point this out, so it helps to put this into perspective.

See, there are actually two types of effort that students can use throughout their studies. There is the right kind of effort, and there is the wrong kind of effort. The right kind earns high grades and success in life. The wrong kind does not.

To demonstrate the difference, let's suppose for a moment that you have just graduated in the field of construction management. As a reward, the state governor has personally asked you to oversee construction of a new, two-hundred-mile freeway system. It will be 16 lanes wide in each direction with helicopter-landing pads to make flying people to hospitals easier in case of accidents. It has exit ramps directly to every school and university parking lot. It has remote lane shifting devices to direct the flow of traffic during accidents or rush hour.

You start your new job with the intent of providing something people will appreciate, and remember you for in the many years to come. You want to make people proud, so you live your work.

To show your investment, you first lease an RV that you can park at the side of the road that you're building so you can always be onsite. For two years, you work seven days a week, twenty hours every day, meticulously laying and pouring your new freeway. You never take a vacation because you want to ensure the job is done right.

Word gets out, and your freeway looks amazing!

Transportation departments from all around the world are hearing about this incredible freeway that you're building, and they send representatives out to see it. You have a ribbon-cutting ceremony. The president of the United States has come to be in the first vehicle that drives onto your freeway.

You cut the ribbon, and the presidential limo drives onto it. Then the limo sinks because, instead of concrete and steel, you have built the entire freeway out of Jello.

Now, did you work hard? Yes!

Did you put in a lot of effort? Yes!

Did you put in the right kind of effort? No, and you're never going to be hired to work in construction management again.

After spending the billions of dollars that it would take to build this kind of a freeway, we cannot say you put forth the right kind of effort because the job was not actually done, and you used the wrong materials.

Let's be clear, there are two ways to approach accomplishing a task. It gets accomplished, or it doesn't.

Any energy that leads to a job getting accomplished, including making the kinds of mistakes we learn from to ultimately accomplish the task, is the right kind of effort. Any energy that doesn't lead to accomplishing the task is the wrong kind of effort. Not only doesn't it lead to accomplishing a task, but it goes an entirely different route to create a different outcome.

I'm not saying this as a means to belittle or degrade any student's efforts. Heaven knows, all students have enough on their plates to survive as they go through this intense journey called *getting a degree*.

I'm saying this because there are ways to fully empower success; ways to partially power that success: and ways to sabotage that success.

The problem is, we get caught in a mindset of confusing the concept of *working hard* for that of *accomplishment*. When we do, we can set ourselves up to not know how to perform projects that bring success. Instead, we practice performing tasks that don't breed accomplishment. Then, because we worked hard, we become stumped as to why we're not getting recognized for performing well.

If you build a freeway out of Jello, you have built it incorrectly. It will not function. It will not last. It will not just fall down, but it will make an absolute mess around you.

No one's going to hire you to build anything ever again. And walking up to your governor to say, "but I put in a lot of effort" isn't going to convince that governor to give you another several billions of dollars to try building a new freeway to see if you can do it right this time. In fact, you will be remembered as the person who built the Jello freeway.

Now, you can be like the oblivious student I had who said, "That's a bad analogy. I never asked to build that freeway." All I can say to that, is that's an even greater recipe for failure and sabotage than putting in the wrong kind of effort. That's an attitude that harbors an extreme form of selfishness that attempts to justify destructive approaches. It doesn't even attempt to acknowledge the concept of taking pride in your work.

It can sound something like this: "So what if my neighbor asked me to watch his dog while he was on vacation, and I fed it rat poison instead of dog food. I never asked to feed his stupid animal."

If you think that kind of snotty attitude is going to open even one window of success to you, you're going to find it quite disappointing when you learn there's no doorman employed to escort you into the foyer of the unemployment office.

Do you seriously think that when you do a job badly, because you didn't ask to do it, that someone's going to want to let you work on the job that you do ask to do?

"After what you did to Bob's dog, no way am I letting you near my own while I'm on vacation. By the way, your Jello driveway is leaking into my grass again. Do I have to sue you again?"

No. You're going to be the person who asks for an opportunity, and the people with the authority to give it to you are going to say amongst themselves, "Anyone but that person."

The purpose of this volume is to help you, the student, to recognize common ways that other students have used to sabotage their abilities that they could otherwise use to learn and find joy in their university-learning endeavors. These are approaches that I have frequently witnessed students employ to build their own Jello freeways. Maybe they can help you, the student, avoid the same trap.

I've seen many students succeed over the years, and I've seen many students fail. In most instances that I've witnessed, I'm sorry to say, it has been because of the sabotage that students inflict upon themselves. I'm not saying that professors can't sabotage students, but students tend to sabotage themselves more without realizing it. As far as how teachers go though, we do have a volume for how professors sabotage students called *Steering Students off Cliffs: 10 Ways Professors Sabotage their Students to Crash and Burn*.

The counsel in this book that you are reading now is intended to help students decipher how to invest the right effort (energy) into your own educational success. Those who practice the right effort in their university studies radiate that energy into their careers and can get rewarded more.

All Elyse and I want to do with this book is help you realize how you can be seen more as someone who does the job with the right effort. The right effort leads to higher grades, greater opportunities, and recognition from mentors and professors without having to ask for it. It leads to good internships and faster movement to gain the best careers once you graduate.

Most of all, it helps you recognize your own value. When you know your true value, that's how you compete for a higher salary in the professional world. You want the most in your grades and your careers? Putting in the right effort, and not sabotaging yourself by putting in the wrong effort, is how you get the most.

Here are ten ways that students can sabotage performing the right effort.

1 — The Syllabus

not reading it

P
r
o
f
e
s
s
o
r
V
i
e
w

"What I envy most about you and everyone else heading back to school is the certainty of it all. You've got a prescribed set of requirements to guide you through the next few years. Focus your energy on the completion of those assignments, and you'll succeed. Guaranteed! Where's my syllabus to guide me through life?"

—Megan McCafferty—
(Author)

Professor Perspective:

This is for all the video game haters (and lovers) out there. I love video games, and I've also been known to play a tabletop game or thirty. There is an excitement to opening a board game, seeing all the pieces, and reading the instructions on what you're supposed to do with those moving parts. I admit, it drives me batty when people make up their own rules and ruin the game because they never actually studied how to play.

In video games, particularly in good ones, I love how clear the objectives are. They often look something like this:

"Clear away or merge these identical pieces."

"Reach this location."

"Locate this item and bring it back to this quest giver."

"Beat up this bully that keeps poking his head out of his cave and stealing our gold."

If you perform the task, you move forward. You get reward. You graduate to the next level. If you get it wrong, you have to keep doing it again until you accomplish the task before you can continue. There is no "oh, you got so close, that's okay, you win the level." And gamers are okay with that. Some people will spend days, weeks, sometimes longer, trying to accomplish one of these tasks just so they can move on to the next objective.

In fact, I have found great amusement in reading video game forums. This is where we find people who can't figure out how to perform a task and then complain about it to other gamers. My favorite is the player who bemoans, "I really hate that we have to perform this quest just to get this piece of armor. They, [the video game makers], should just give it to us." The response always invites an answer from veteran gamers of: "Ooh, and maybe they can give you a version of the game where you win just by turning it on." Yes. Believe it or not, there are people who do not want to have to perform the goals that are the very reason the game exists in the first place.

My next favorite comments are from people who don't read the instructions and come to the forums asking, "How do you play this?" To which, someone responds, "Read the instructions. They tell you exactly what to do."

As someone who loves games, I can always tell which people to turn to for advice on how to play better. It's based entirely upon who has clearly read the instructions. I can also tell which opposing players will be easy to beat in competition, because of how clear it has become that they have not read the instructions.

The worst performing gamers—as well as the most unreliable and untrustworthy—are those who don't study the instructions of the game before playing.

Now, interesting comparison, I see a very similar effect in the classroom when students sign up for a class and then don't read the syllabus.

As a student and a teacher, I can genuinely say that almost the biggest way that you can sabotage yourself in any university course is to disregard the instruction book called the syllabus.

I understand that it's easy for every syllabus to look the same. There was a time that these manuals were typically one-page long and different from one class to the next, but then we became a society where people blame others, and universities have become customer service hubs that don't want to get sued. So, the university administrators have begun bloating every syllabus of every class with the same campus-wide policies, such as plagiarism, or offices or Websites that offer many types of student support. It seems every syllabus has become a uniform and required manual that the professor can add individual class information to, but only after others, who are not even in the class, already have. What used to be a one or two-page document has become 32 pages.

I admit, that's not cool because it scares the student off from reading the syllabus. However, the syllabus still contains individualized instruction for students to succeed, and failing to read it does affect your ability to fully perform in the class.

There are certain attitudes that correlate between a student's willingness to read and study a syllabus and the rest of their conduct in the classroom and their personal studies.

I will tell you right now, nothing alerts a professor to a pupil's laziness more than a student who has demonstrated they have not read the syllabus.

Ah! That sounds harsh, doesn't it? But guess what? That's the truth. Nothing shows a student's lack of investment in a classroom more than refusing (that's right refusing) to read a syllabus. If you learn anything from this book, learn this: a student who doesn't read a syllabus is a lazy, underperforming student. If you think otherwise, consider then that students who don't read the syllabus are typically not exceptional in their work (even if they technically get high grades). If you are one who has earned an A in a class without reading the syllabus, I'm going to tell you a secret: Unless your professor was trying to be a friend rather than a teacher, you are not your professor's favorite student, nor do you have their support for remarkable opportunity. Why? Because we see the true attitudes you adopted when you disregarded the simple instruction booklet called the syllabus. It shows in your learning conduct.

For example, classes require students to read large amounts of study material. It is not uncommon for a class to require a text book or multiple text books. Classes can require hundreds, even thousands of pages of reading material for a student to succeed.

The syllabus is the smallest test possible that students can take to evaluate their true investment in the class. If a student cannot read a syllabus, they are not going to invest in reading other material needed to excel throughout the semester. If you're not willing to read the instruction for the class as a whole, you set yourself up to misunderstand that entire purpose of the course, and you will incorrectly apply the details of your curriculum. It is the details that set apart high-earning grades from lower earning grades (or even a failing grade).

Students who don't read the syllabus often start the class in confusion. Students who read the syllabus understand where the teacher is coming from, what is expected, and what the path is. Students who don't read the syllabus can take on attitudes of blaming everyone but themselves for their own lack of preparation.

In my classroom, students who don't read the syllabus are more likely to misunderstand important concepts. I have seen many students fail final exams because they went the entire semester hearing all the details of the course, but never learning the purpose of those details because they didn't read the syllabus.

Students who don't read the syllabus tend not to understand the purpose of assignments nor how they work together—even to the detriment of missing due dates.

Students who don't read the syllabus set themselves up to think they don't need to read other instructional material such as assignment rubric and description.

Students who don't read the syllabus can be tempted to disrespect their own peers in the class because they haven't learned how to interact with those who did read it.

Those who don't read the syllabus contribute to wasting class time, and that is something professors notice. By not reading, students will too often ask questions that demand immediate time-consuming answers and can stall the progression of everyone else in the room, all because that student couldn't take the time to read the instruction book given to them on the first day of class. This has led to the all powerful mantra that professors repeat in classrooms everywhere: "It's in the syllabus."

What we're really saying is, "You already have the answer. Why are you wasting my time?"

Other than anti-learning attitudes that people can enter a classroom with, nothing sabotages a student's ability to succeed in the university setting more than not reading the syllabus, because it begins a habit and a mindset of believing you can keep ignoring instructional material throughout the semester.

Because this is so important to a student's success, I'll say it again. Nothing shows a student's lack of investment in a classroom more than refusing (that's right refusing) to read a syllabus. If you learn anything from this book, learn this (and I have no problem stating this): A student who doesn't read a syllabus is a lazy, underperforming student. If you don't like hearing that, tough! Do you want to succeed? Or do you want to feel like you're being tortured all semester because you don't know how to interact with the class? That's the power of the syllabus.

To overcome sabotaging your scores, you need to understand that students can be the most destructive force to their grades above anyone else.

Those who don't read the syllabus train themselves to cut corners that should not be cut. Sure, these students may graduate, and they may get points technically, but they will never be the first choice for the teacher to support. That might not seem like much to students who don't care, but consider this: The university is a practice ground for attitudes that contribute to real-world success. If you practice cutting corners in the university, you will demonstrate that you are a person who tries the same in your career; you will never be the best at what you do; and others will see it.

Something as simple as refusing to read a syllabus, sets a student on a path to be okay with not understanding their environment, and seeking sub-par potential.

Harsh? Yes.

True? Moreso.

Student Perspective:

Whether it's your very first week of school as a bright-eyed, hopeful freshman or your very last day of class as a disheveled, exhausted senior, we're all aware of what the first week of coursework entails: The syllabus. These handy-dandy guides to the classroom come in many different forms. Maybe your professor posted their syllabus solely online, or perhaps they printed it for you in a stapled stack of papers that would get lost in your backpack. Maybe they walked the entire class through a long PowerPoint filled with stuffy words and cringy memes. No matter what form your syllabus comes in, each class will have one.

It may be tempting that first week of attendance to say: "Oh, it's the first week. It will be fine if I skip. I can just get caught up online if I ever need to see the syllabus. It's not a big deal!" Let me tell you, from someone who has been in your shoes, that is a bad idea. Trust me, I've been there. The first week of classes is hard enough without adding hours upon hours of boring instructions and grading rules. However, reading the syllabus could be the difference between succeeding in that class and crashing and burning.

You might be asking: "Elyse, how could one boring document make that much of a difference?"

Let me tell you a story that happened to me in one of my last semesters of school that proved to me how important reading that little document was, and how it really could save my entire grade. I was in a higher-level language course, which means all of the students taking it had gone through their fair share of first-day orientations. As usual, we were given a syllabus. Some of the students took the professor's advice and read through it. Others just stuffed it in their backpacks, never to be seen again. No one thought much of the syllabus until it came to reckoning day. It was the week before Christmas break, and our professor had just informed us when our final would be: Saturday, the very last day of finals, at 4:00 in the afternoon.

It was like a nuclear bomb went off in that classroom, which was hilarious, seeing as this was an American Sign Language course. The classroom was typically silent from complete immersion in practicing the language, but it now erupted with people throwing tantrums. Several students were near tears as they angrily argued with the professor that there had to be a different day or time, they could take the exam. The professor explained that, because it was an in-person exam, it would just not be possible, as she would be signing the test while the rest of us wrote down our answers.

Another uproar occurred. Several students loudly exclaimed that this wasn't fair to drop on us without warning, as several people had scheduled flights or other holiday plans in the works. The professor just listened to these exasperated students before slowly and calmly telling us, "The date of the final hasn't been changed from the first day of school. It was in the Syllabus."

Now, let me tell you, that you could hear a pin drop in that classroom. It became very clear that it wasn't the professor's nor even the department's fault for the ruined holiday plans, but rather the nearly seventy percent of the classroom that hadn't carefully checked their syllabus.

Most of the time, reading the syllabus won't be so dramatic of a choice. However, I can promise you that document will be your best friend. It will give you a much needed glimpse into your professors and how they run their classrooms; help you know their late work policy; and keep you in the know of difficult assignments, weeks before you get them. Don't be a student forced to miss your family Christmas trip because you didn't look at the syllabus. Give it a read, I promise it won't take more than a few minutes to get through. Keep it close, rely on it, and you'll be surprised to see how far your good friend the syllabus will get you.

The syllabus is the key to knowing how to locate the majority of resources that can make your studies easier. Colleges want their students to succeed, and they have given a variety of ways to do so. To figure out what resources are available to you, refer to that handy-dandy syllabus. Sure, you can look around for extra help on your own. You can find people you like (or maybe even just tolerate) and form a study group. Even then, one of the biggest mistakes a student can make is ignoring their syllabus and its instruction to locate helpful tools.

Too often, we think we can get by on our own, and that we know better. This can lead to misinformation, drowning in work, and feeling lost and behind in our courses. The syllabus is your life vest when that happens. So, keep that syllabus in a safe dust-free place that's available when you need it. Take advantage of that document, and I promise you a helpful boost on your courses, degree, and—most importantly—your life as a student.

S
t
u
d
e
n
t

V
i
e
W

2 — Smile and Nod

not participating

Professor View

"Personal participation is the universal principle of knowing."

—Michael Polanyi—
(Polymath)

Professor Perspective:

Sometimes, the teachers that we learn the best from and who leave us with the lessons that we remember most are those we can't stand. Sometimes, that's good. Sometimes, it's bad. Like when my zoology 1010 professor would stand at the front of class before tests and say, "Study these pages, but don't worry about this information because it's not on the test." Then the test was on everything he specifically told us not to study. I believe there's a special place in hell for that kind of teacher.

However, then he stopped lecture one day because two students wouldn't shut up, and he said, "You know, the nice thing about college is that if you don't want to be here, there's doors." That taught me that my education was in my hands.

My zoology professor had 250 students in his lecture hall. I don't have nearly that many in my classroom.

Hey, remember that time you went to the movie theater to see that one movie? You know, that really cool one that everyone couldn't wait to see, and it seemed like it would never come out

P
r
o
f
e
s
s
o
r

V
i
e
W

fast enough? Remember when you got there, how you pulled your sound-proofing headphones over your ears; drew your sleep mask over your eyes; you curled up under your blanket; and went to sleep in the fancy theater recliners? Remember that?

No? You never did that, you say? That would be a waste of money, you say?

Oh.

Hey! Remember that time you signed up for a class, and you smiled at the teacher when he looked at you, and then you nodded whenever you agreed with what he said? Remember when you didn't agree with what he said, but you nodded anyway because it made you look like you understood the lesson? Remember that?

Yes, you do. Don't lie! I'm shaking an angry, old-person fist at you now in case you couldn't tell.

Here's the problem with that. It's one of the worst ways students can sabotage themselves, and not just in the classroom. Of all the forms of sabotage that this book discusses, this is perhaps the one that trains a person not to get involved in their classroom community most.

When you smile and nod, but don't honestly speak to actually participate, you create the foundation of a habit that avoids being involved, being seen, and being heard—all behaviors that are what getting degrees are all about.

Here's where this is an issue for students entering careers. It doesn't matter what you study or what job you get, smile-and-nod attitudes don't get rewarded. In the chance that they do get noticed, it's for nothing more than to be a supervisor's personal pin cushion. Personal pin cushions do the work that managers don't want to do.

The classroom provides many ways to hear your voice and to participate. Being involved is the best way to practice hearing your ideas that can benefit others. The educational setting is the best place to practice being involved. No other setting is designed to cater to such grand practice, while providing many minds to question you and help you tighten your ideas. It lets you realize that you do have something to contribute, and that your input can influence others. Using your voice empowers others and you.

To be fair, I have absolutely no problem speaking in front of groups. I am confident in using my voice. Speaking publicly does not intimidate me. I can make people laugh, cry, or both. I can inspire. I can drive points into messages that can cause people to want to act upon what I say.

It didn't always used to be that way though. A long, long time ago in a community far, far away, I was made fun of for who I was and what I had to say. I was bullied. I was silenced. I was berated. I became a punching bag for other people. Teachers didn't see me. Adults made harmful assumptions about me. Hateful classmates saw me though and so did abusive friends.

At one time, it was ingrained into me to be afraid of speaking for fear of how it would invite others to behave towards me. Speaking in front of people made me sick.

At 16 years old, I got a summer job in another community, as an amusement park ride operator. This job put a microphone in my hand and surrounded me with opportunity to use, to hear, and to see my voice affect others. Not long after, I was training people to amplify their own voices. A few, short years later, I was performing for large crowds and lines of people (with and without a microphone). I developed volume. I got unlimited opportunity to speak to and to entertain people either one-on-one or in groups.

I started writing and performing comedy routines, I performed and sang in lead roles on stage. I taught classes. I went to college (after dropping out of high school). I went to grad school. Each class I took was a community within a larger community where I learned voices shaped discussion. I took public speaking, so I could learn to speak to audiences. I took classes in studying group dynamics and interpersonal relationships, all so I could understand interactions with others better. I studied journalism in great depth, which pushed me out to meet and interview new people and then write about them. It earned me a communication degree in journalism.

At the same time, I was taking writing courses to explore my literary voice, which simultaneously earned me a second degree in creative writing.

I have fully witnessed the dichotomy of once being physically petrified to speak and now being completely comfortable to do so at a moment's invitation. On top of that, I teach people how to tap into their own unique voices.

Here's the amazing power of voices: the more you use yours, the more powerful it becomes. There is an energy that builds in individuals who use their voices. It's like their own personal battery. It's easy to feel safe with a battery that's empty, so long as you take no behavior to fill that battery by using your voice. We're only uncomfortable with it when we are put in a position that would contribute to charging it. The problem is, a dead battery may feel safe, but a dead battery never empowers personal success nor other people's. Any time you speak, you add to that battery's storage, and that's where we find the power to take opportunity.

Saying "hi" to a stranger can be debilitating for some people. The first time you say "hi" to a stranger can be difficult. The fiftieth can be difficult, but not as much as the first. The more you say "hi" to people, the easier it becomes. The more you say it, the more you warm up to follow up words such as, "I like your coat" or "thank you." We can even warm up to conversation with "How are you?" or "Where are you from?"

You want to know where one of the perfect classrooms are to learn how to speak? A park or city bench. Pretty much every person you see doesn't know who you are. You'll never see them again if you make a mistake.

Simply start by saying nothing at all, just wave or nod a friendly salutation to them. This is a nonverbal approach to warming up your ability to begin vocally projecting. Do it enough, and you'll find yourself naturally moving onto the next step, which is to start saying, "Hi." Just say, "Hi." Even just saying this one word, will empower how you say it, and how you take in others' responses to it. Some will say "hi" back. Some will ignore you. Some might stop and ask you how your day is. Some might inquire what you're doing. Tell them, "I'm practicing not being afraid to talk to people." Who could get mad at that? A bench where people walk by is the perfect place to speak to people.

Then take it to the next step, ask a stranger for directions:

"Is there a library around here?"

"How do I get to Walmart?"

"Do you know what time the bus comes?"

Even if you know the answers, ask. This process isn't about having the answers, it's about practicing using your voice and seeing how others interact with it. Give random compliments to people as they pass by, watch them smile. "I love your hat! Where did you get it?" People love compliments. Be careful about complimenting people about their bodies though. "I love your hair" can creep strangers out. Save those compliments for people you're more comfortable saying them to. Watch people smile when you give those compliments, because, in that moment, you have made that person feel good. It's small, but you can see the power of your voice through other people's smiles.

How does this apply to a college student though?

Because each class is designed to help you focus your voice into a conversation. Like the park bench practice, it's going to be difficult to give your first answers. It's even difficult on some students to say "yes" or "no" when a teacher asks them a surprise question. Here are three answers that will help make even the most frightened of students vocally stronger: *Yes, no,* and *I don't know.*

Every teacher's inquiries can be acknowledged in class with these responses. Where students often make mistakes with their voices is they believe they have to know the answer or look stupid in front of the class. The reality is, all the other students in your class are just happy they didn't get called on.

Some teachers can get pushy: "Why don't you know." That's where the power of "I don't know" comes in. You don't have to like the answer, but you're using your voice. Somewhere in your brain, you might just ask yourself, "why don't I know" and then make it a point to go find out on your own.

By the way, if you get a question from a teacher that catches you off guard, you can always ask the teacher, "come back to me" and buy yourself some time. When, and if, the teacher remembers to come back to you, you can still say "I don't know" if you don't know. If a teacher gets mad at you for that, that is on the teacher, not on you, and your classmates will recognize that. Some teachers are just jerks.

Never let a jerk professor's ego get in the way of your perseverance to magnify your voice. Remember that and keep saying "I don't know" if you don't know. If a jerk teacher wants you to know so badly, and you don't know the answer, she can give you the answer so that you do know. That's part of how teaching works.

What's happening here is that you're filling your vocal battery, but it doesn't happen by just smiling and nodding at your teacher when she invites your participation. If you enter the classroom smiling and nodding, you are likely to leave the class smiling and nodding, and that doesn't help you test how strong your stances are. However, enter a class using simple words to participate, adding to your vocal battery, and you leave the class a bit more confident in your voice and philosophies.

The charge generally begins with using simple words, but eventually it will evolve into sharing your thoughts or challenging other people's ideologies. When you have twelve to fifteen weeks in a classroom with the same people every day, it's like being on the park bench, but with people you know (and they're just trying to charge their vocal batteries too).

The more you discover your thoughts, the more you try to vocalize them. The more you vocalize, the more you'll find yourself warming up to use other responses that go beyond *yes*, *no*, and *I don't know*. This is how vocal confidence builds. Where using your voice fuels your battery, confidence keeps you from spending the energy that you've stored. Sadly, not everything is that simple, right?

Unfortunately, you can spend vocal battery charge when you make a comment you regret, and you tell yourself that maybe you could say it differently next time. While this may eat away at your charge, because you've already experienced what juicing up that vocal battery feels like, it's easier to rebuild that energy. This helps you build power not only in your voice, but it increases a resistance within you against feeling like you should be silenced.

The university setting is about building up the energy in that battery that fuels your voice. University degrees were never intended to teach silence. Their entire purpose is to promote interaction with others. You learn your discipline; you magnify your voice in that discipline; you take your voice into your career where you enhance the discipline of that career; and you influence your peers for the better. People who don't practice using their voices miss out on many opportunities that further success. The reality is that bigger paychecks go to people with stronger charges in their voice batteries, and university settings are designed specifically to help charge those batteries.

Consider this, it takes an average of four years to earn a 120-semester-credit-hour degree. That's roughly 40 courses; 600 weeks of classes; an average of 1,500 different sessions; 1,800 hours that you will meet with fellow students and teachers. That's a lot of time to practice fueling your battery with people who want to help you fuel it, or it's a lot of time to avoid charging it.

When we smile and nod, we don't use our voices, we don't fuel our batteries with energy that we can take into our careers. It's not a matter of being introverted or extroverted. Many introverts are excellent at using their voices but will be the first to tell you they will be happy to get home where they can be in their own climate.

When you take a class. Smile-and-nod may get you out of being put on the spot, but it doesn't expand your voice. Your voice is where the pay raises and promotions are. Instead, speak. Even if it's saying *yes*, *no*, and *I don't know*. Just saying these have more influence on you to feel more confident in sharing your ideas eventually than if you just smile and nod.

When discovering your voice, there is power in "I don't know" over saying nothing at all, even if you're nodding while you're saying nothing.

Proofessors, Voice, W

Student Perspective:

Now, it's kind of a big understatement to say that life as a student is overwhelming. Trust me. I had days where I forgot to eat, sleep, or even check in with my family. Here are just a few stressors that a student's life entails: Paying rent on time, making rent money, keeping up with homework, having a social life, staying healthy, and having good grades.

Because of these many stressors hefted upon full-time students, we understandably start to develop coping skills to deal with the pressure that is crushing us from all sides. Sometimes, that's taking an early morning yoga class, watching a comfort tv show, stuffing your face with two-dollar Taco Bell burritos while you listen to Mr. Brightside, or hanging out with close friends to chat. However, not going into how healthy (or unhealthy) these example coping mechanisms are, there are some things we do to get by that can greatly hinder our success as a college student. One of these more popular ones is having a smile-and-nod attitude.

Now, what exactly is the good, old, smile-and-nod attitude? Well, it can come in many different forms and situations, but mainly it's putting on a blank face and just going with the flow. This means taking things as they come and not really caring about the how or why of the situation.

At a glance, that may not seem so overly bad. After all, you're still going into class and putting forth effort, so why does it matter if you just breeze by without really caring? The reason is because unless you're in a 101 Yoga class where the goal is to learn how to cleanse your mind and reach full meditation, you're not going to be able to just breeze by. It might work for an assignment or two, or maybe even a full class, but eventually you're going to wake up from your blissful ignorance and realize you know nothing about your classes, or even what you're doing in college. Your drive will be gone faster than a tater tot in a room full of first graders. So, how do we avoid falling into this attitude? The first step is recognizing the signs.

I mainly see the old smile-and-nod in freshman and seniors, but both for very different reasons. For freshman, the attitude comes out of a will to not stand out.

We've all been there.

It's the first day of a class that you're really worried about. You're getting all your pencils ready for notes, and you are determined to put your best foot forward. Things seem to be going well but then, whether it be the first day or midway through the semester, you hit a block. Something doesn't make sense, an assignment wasn't explained clearly, or you feel like the professor contradicted themselves. What do you do? You glance around at the rest of the classroom and see students dutifully writing down their notes, staring at the professor and sometimes (most terrifyingly) smiling and laughing as though the professor had shared some secret joke just with them.

That's when the panic sets in. You try to school your features, because if you look even the slightest bit confused, everyone is going to think that you don't understand. I mean, you don't, but the only thing worse than not understanding is having anyone *know* that you don't understand.

So, you take a deep breath, you look down at your notes, and you fade out. Life becomes blissful and quiet. Maybe you're thinking about the dinner you're going to have that night; or the movie you watched the evening before; or the sad little ant crawling along on the carpet by your feet. Whatever it is that keeps you occupied, by the time you zone back in, you're even more confused. So, you fade back out, and, before you know it, class is over, your notebook is blank, and your mind even more so.

From my own observations, this same effect happens with more senior students except, instead of being due to confusion (which still happens mind you), it comes more from a boredom aspect.

You're in your high level English class and they're discussing Hamlet for the umpteenth time. Not only have you read Hamlet like two hundred and eighty four times, but you've seen the David Tennant version. So, you're pretty much an expert. Because you're confident in your knowledge, you fade out, thinking you have far better things to worry about. By the time your brain is back in class the professor is discussing how Laertes is actually a metaphor for the Atlantic Ocean, Hamlet is meant to be a self-insert character, and Ophelia never truly existed at all.

Your mind quickly gets overwhelmed, so what do you do? You smile, and you nod. Professor asks if you understand it? Smile and nod. The professor starts discussing the pros and cons of Anti-capitalism in the 1600s? Smile and nod.

Look, we've all been these students before. Whether you're too afraid to look stupid, or too far in to back out now, everyone has fallen back on the smile-and-nod attitude. However, we've also then all felt the repercussions. Despite the fear of looking stupid, you often look more so in the future with smile-and-nod. Smiling and nodding will only get you so far until you're asked a question or have to do an assignment that everyone else seems to understand. It's then that, because you breezed by in class, you're stuck up the creek without a paddle. So, how does one avoid this mindset before it sets in?

One of the first keys to battling the smile and nod is to lose the self-conscious attitude. One of my favorite quotes from my mother is "No one is thinking about you. They're all too worried thinking about themselves." So, if you're confused in class, ask. It's not like anyone is going to spend days thinking about your question and how prevalent it was. If asking in front of the class isn't your favorite, write down your questions as they come, and then talk to the professor after lecture or during their office hours. Honestly, that's what they're there for, to help you understand and succeed. So, take advantage of them.

Chances are also very high that if you have a question, someone around you has the same one. And—hey—even if you're the only one who seems to have that question, or you sound dumb, who cares? It's your education you should be worried about, not the people around you! If speaking out in class is still not really your speed, ask your classmates for a bit of help. If it's a quick question, or you just missed part of a sentence, chances are that one of your peers has written things down and would be able to clarify for you.

The second key to battling smile and nod is to not let yourself get caught up in the same old. With so many different classes and professors you're going to be repeating some material. If I had to tell you how many times I read Frankenstein in college I think it would actually blow your mind. However, fading away in class and not paying attention isn't helpful to anyone. Despite similar (or even identical) course material, you're in a different class with different teachers, curriculum, and students. This means there will be something new to learn, and smiling and nodding could cause you to miss it.

For instance, the first time I read Frankenstein we focused on the moral. The second time was more about its place as a British literature book. Third time was about its gothic themes, and the fourth time was all about gothic feminism. It's the same book, but taught in four different classes with their own eye-opening themes and facts. This is the same in all methods of learning. Whether you're applying a math formula; a different way learning more about a scientific theory; or even another technique to make a clay pot, your class has something to teach you.

So, next time you're fading out, you're confused, or you don't think something is worth your time, zero back in.

Oftentimes, one of the biggest reasons I've seen students lose their drive is because they adopt this smile-and-nod mentality and stop caring about what they're learning. Despite the stress of looking stupid, or being bored, take a deep breath and hone back in on your lesson, assignment, or discussion. You won't regret it when you're taking the final, and your brain pulls more than a big blank.

S
t
u
d
e
n
t

V
i
e
W

3 — Dumb Questions
asking them

P
r
o
f
e
s
s
o
r

V
,
l
e
W

"Someone said to me, 'Hey, what's it like kissing Marilyn Monroe?' I said, 'It's like kissing Hitler. What are you doing asking me such a stupid question?'"

—Tony Curtis—
(Actor)

Professor Perspective:

As a teacher, I'm supposed to say there are no dumb questions, but that's not true. Dumb questions litter University classrooms.

Many years ago, I worked at an amusement park as a ride operator. Sometimes, a ride would stop working and we'd have to close it while maintenance worked to fix the problem. On more than one occasion, I found myself sitting in front of broken-down rides, such as a 150-foot Ferris wheel. I'd carry out a big sign. On one side, the sign would say: "We're sorry. This ride is temporarily closed." On the other side of the sign, it would say: "We're sorry. This ride is temporarily closed." Then, I'd stand beside the sign to tell approaching guests, "I'm sorry. This ride is temporarily closed."

Sometimes, there'd be banging on the ride from maintenance crew pounding on some stubborn mechanical part that needed a good beating to get it working again.

So, guests walked up to a ride that didn't have a single person waiting in line. They'd read the sign: "We're sorry. This ride is temporarily closed." I would say, "I'm sorry. This ride is temporarily closed." The guest would look at the empty and non-moving ride.

The maintenance crew would be "Bang! Bang! Bang!" The guest would look at the ride and its unpopulated queue line. Again, the guest would look at the sign: "We're sorry. This ride is temporarily closed." They'd listen to me tell another guest, "I'm sorry. This ride is temporarily closed." They'd look to the sign: "We're sorry. This ride is temporarily closed." All the time, "Bang! Bang! Bang!" on the ride.

Then they'd look at me and ask: "Are you open?"

That's a dumb question. He ignored his community and environment, then gave no regard to the tools that were abundantly provided beforehand to answer his highly anticipated question.

Stupid questions spur from when people don't prepare themselves before asking. I'm not talking about questions that need additional clarification. I'm talking about a student who has the tools that already answer anticipated potential questions, but then that student ignores those tools. Rather than ask questions that can help them overcome what they don't know, they ask questions that demonstrate that they are not involved in their community.

This matters because teachers remember this lack of investment when it comes time for them to award points for participation at the end of the semester. If they have to choose between giving a higher grade to a student who was involved in the community and a lower grade to a student who was not involved. I promise, they will assure that the involved student gets more grade recognition than the student who ignored their community. Therein, lies the student self-sabotage.

In the professional world, ignoring your community and shirking your responsibility, will get that responsibility handed to someone else.

It might seem common sense that if you want to learn, you need to show up and participate, but there are more students than I'd like to say I've encountered who seem to think that the best way to learn is to ignore the class until their assignment becomes a reality at the last possible moment. In doing so, these student often don't realize that they are, in fact, harming their own opportunities to succeed.

A teacher only has so much time before a deadline to answer questions, so they enlist various tools to help answer them. When a student ignores those tools then asks questions that demonstrate the student ignored those tools, it robs time from the members of their classroom community who did prepare themselves with those tools.

After four weeks working on a particular assignment, I once emailed a class to remind them of its upcoming due date. The email read: "This is a reminder that we are finishing up our synthesis essays this week. They are due Friday by midnight." I promptly received a reply from a student asking, "Hi professor, I was just curious, what was our assignment and when is it due?"

Now, this student had a syllabus with the deadline. They had an online calendar that informed him weeks in advance of this deadline. He had a grading rubric, assignment description, and multiple discussions, to remind him all about the assignment and when it was due. In fact, he ignored the email that stated "this is the assignment and this is when it's due," he replied to it with, "what's the assignment and when is it due."

That's a stupid question. It was a demonstration that the student had ignored his community and its tools for four weeks.

To answer his dumb question, I simply copied my original email, which he had already replied to in asking this question, and pasted it as a reply because it seemed nicer than saying, "Flush your stupid and repeat!"

On another occassion, I spent an entire class period, meticulously explaining a particular concept only to have a regularly inattentive student ask in the last 15 seconds of class, "Will you be showing us how that concept works?" I watched a classroom of students' eyes roll at him.

Rather than say, "Flush your stupid and repeat, what do you think we've been doing for the last hour?" I simply said, "Ask another student if you can look at their notes from today." In his lack of attentiveness to the answer he had just received, the student expected me to do the entire lecture again in our remaining ten seconds of class.

When a student makes the assumption that a teacher has the time to drop everything, and repeat an entire lecture just for that student, because the student ignored his community, that leads to a stupid question topped with a fat, dollop of whipped, unrealistic expectation and a big, red maraschino cherr-"duh."

However, as truly unprepared as these questions are, they are still not the dumbest question that I've encountered (not even close).

Here is the dumbest question: A student misses a day of lecture, then comes up and asks, "I wasn't here yesterday. Did I miss anything?"

P

r

o

f

e

s

s

o

r

V

,

i

e

W

The answer that always jumps to the front of my mind is: "Nooo! You weren't here, so we all went to a baseball game."

For some reason, even by the time students reach university-level status, many haven't grasped that when they miss a day of lecture, the classroom community and environment goes on. Then these students want to know how they can get the information they missed as though they've ever once had a teacher repeat the entire lecture just for them rather than direct them to ask another student to borrow their notes.

This kind of lack of prescence in their own communities can drive students to ask some of the most unprepared and stupid questions since Stockton Rush, the man who said that "at some point, safety is just pure waste," would later ask "Hey, anyone want to go see the Titanic with me?"

Combine unprepared questions with, "Well, what's the assignment that's due tomorrow?" And the answer becomes one about demonstrating how the student asking that question doesn't deserve an A in the class.

Any time that you have access to answers that were specifically prepared for you beforehand, but you choose to ignore them out of your own laziness, lays a path to asking stupid questions.

Professors have limited time, and that's why you'll sometimes get answers like: "It's in the syllabus." Or "did you read the rubric." Or "You'll need to borrow notes." It's not that we don't want to answer your questions, it's just that we don't like being expected to care more about a student getting their answers than they do.

It takes teachers far more time to prepare and deliver answers than it does for a student to read them. When a student can't be bothered to put in the minimal work to receive and meditate on those answers, that acts as a megaphone to the teacher that the student doesn't care about the teacher's investment in that student.

It's not a matter of asking a stupid question then. It's an insult to the teacher and the community, and it can deny points in the final grade, because your behavior told your professor, "I do not care about my own studies nor your investment in me." Teachers remember that when it's time to evaluate class participation points.

It will prompt our own teacher-questions, such as: "Does this student deserve the same grade as my involved students?"

What makes a question stupid isn't that it's because of the topic, or because the student doesn't know something. It becomes a stupid question when it makes the person asking it look lazy and uninvolved in their own success. If you have answers at your fingertips; if you have a support system and community of allies in your corner; and if you ignore all that, it becomes apparent in what you ask—and that's the formula to a stupid question. That laziness will not earn points, allies nor support—because it's difficult to support someone who shows little to no regard for that support.

Don't cofuse stupid with ignorance though. We can be ignorant of information and get over it by asking questions (prepared questions). That's not what makes a stupid question.

A teacher does not become subconsciously biased against a student's performance in a class when they ask, "I know you answered this here, but can you clarify this information for me" because we can see the student is invested and on their way to a potential A.

When we get an email from a student that asks "what's our assignment and when is it due," and its three hours before the deadline, and after several weeks of preparation, discussion and provision of tools to assist the student, we think: "Do you know how blatantly you had to ignore your community to ask that question?"

And I promise, those little subconscious responses stick in a teacher's mind when we start awarding participation points.

That's what makes them stupid questions. That's how so many students sabotage their grades. Because they are training themselves not to be part of their own supportive community. Turn your back on your community and you will ask stupid questions because you don't get to know your allies. That will cause you to lose support.

Don't prepare yourself, you ask stupid questions. Ask stupid questions, and you set yourself up to ignore your own tools. Ignore your own tools, and the professor sees a student who cuts corners and expects the teacher to care more about the student's success than the student does.

There is no success to be had in that approach.

Student Perspective:

Okay, now we've all heard the age old saying "there are no dumb questions." Now, I hate to be the one to break it to you, but that's wrong. There are *definitely* dumb questions. In fact, some of the dumbest questions you will ever hear will be in your college classes. Now, I'm not meaning questions that you think are beneath you or questions that you already have the answer to. Those are going to happen, and that doesn't make them dumb questions. Some theories, ideas, and facts take longer to get into people's heads than others. Not knowing something doesn't make you dumb, needing a bit more clarification doesn't make you dumb neither. No, What makes a question dumb is if you answer *yes* to one or more of the following questions that make the following acronym B.A.D.:

Has my question been answered by class resources **B**efore?
Am I straying into my own, personal **A**dventure?
Am I lighting off a **D**ud question?

This helpful acronym **B.A.D.** can help you make sure you're not the one asking the stupid questions in class that make all of the students roll their eyes and wish that they were taking Biology 509 instead of listening to you talk.

The first step is B (Before), such as: Has my question been answered by class resources **B**efore now?

One of the most frustrating things in any class is when someone asks a question that the professor just answered or is clearly written on the board. If you're anything like me though, when you're getting a lot of information thrown at you at once, you like to know things immediately. It takes too much time to sort through things when the professor is speaking faster than Usain Bolt can run, and the white board is looking more and more like ancient Greek. Sometimes, all you will need is a clarifying question such as "Professor, I'm sorry did you say anthropomorphic or Anthropometric?" or "Is the number you wrote 122 or 722?" Questions like these aren't stupid. In fact, odds are someone else will have the same question.

People presenting this kind of question usually aren't asking because they're stressed or frazzled (or maybe they are a little), but it's mostly to clarify instruction in the moment.

However, sometimes questions get asked with next to zero thought process to them. These are questions like, "Hey, is the Southwest Florida Eagle found in America?" or "When you said you would be splitting us into random groups, will we be able to pick our partners?"

These in-the-moment questions usually happen when you aren't paying attention to the lecture at-hand. Trust me, I've been there. I've faded off and realized I missed something very important that the professor definitely brought up already. In that case, take a moment to check the information already in your notes and see if they clear up your confusion. If not, don't be afraid to say, "I think I missed something you said, do you have time to summarize what you just said, or should I wait until after class to ask?" This puts the responsibility on the teacher to choose if your question is good to answer with the time the class period offers (even ask if anyone else needs that information), or politely say to you, "Well, let's talk after class," without putting you on the spot.

However, if you're confused in the moment and you haven't been taking notes and you haven't been reviewing other course materials, asking even these kinds of questions, even if they feel like they're for in-the-moment clarification, you will just waste the rest of the class's time like a bunch of Karens trying to choose what to sing at a karaoke club—and the class was probably paying attention. That's when you should consider meeting with the professor outside of the classroom on how to clear up the confusion.

Here are some hacks though that I've found you can ask if this happens to you no matter what. Ask your question when there's a big break to do so and start the question with: "I know you already discussed this, but I'm just clarifying that…"

If there's no chance or break in lecture to pose your question, ask a fellow student: "Hey. Sorry. I didn't catch what she said. Is the exam on penguins due on Tuesday night or Wednesday night?" If that one fails you as well, you can always take the pathway of shame up to the professor's desk after class and ask your redundant questions then. Professors are usually more understanding of dumb questions when you're not wasting precious class time.

Next up in the acronym is **A** for **A**dventure: Am I straying into my own, personal **A**dventure?

Make sure your questions coincide with the material and current topic? I've been in some really interesting classes before—ones where the professor and students got so animated that we started the class talking about Lais (a type of poetry) and ended the class talking about all six wives of King Henry (two completely unrelated, but potentially enjoyable, topics).

At first glance, questions asking about interesting topics or clarifications don't seem dumb. However, you can quickly enter the slippery slope of questions that you don't really need the answers to in that moment. If your upcoming test is all about modern fantasy writers, you don't really need to query about what the first science fiction book was, because you know how Google works (write your question down and go ask it later.) No matter how interesting that is and how far you can reach to try to get to that answer, I've found that there will always be time for the fun or extra queries eventually. If you're in a crunch, focus on what you need to ask first to avoid being labeled as a dumb inquirer.

Lastly, in **B.A.D.**, is **D** for **D**ud: Am I lighting off a **D**ud question?

Most of the time you are asking because you need an answer—that's part of the definition of a genuine question. However, there are many reasons for someone to ask what I like to call a dud question or something you don't really need the answer to.

Sometimes, dud questions are asked to distract. Maybe you know the professor is about to talk about something boring or bring up an assignment you're avoiding, so you pose a question to delay this. These questions are meant to derail the professor. As useful as this seems at the moment, I can promise you Professor Johnson will remember that test eventually or get to that topic you hate. You're just avoiding the inevitable and wasting class time by asking questions like this.

Dud questions are also asked because of something called participation points. Lots of classes use these handy, little points to grade you on how active you are in class discussions. For even some of the most extroverted students, these participation points can be daunting to achieve. Because of that, some students find themselves asking redundant or dumb questions in the hope that they'll at least get their points for the day.

However, although you need your points, you need them and your questions to mean something. Your professor will remember your part in the discussion if you ask a question like: "Professor, in your opinion would you consider war good or bad" when you're class is discussing how to triangulate the location of Venus in your Astronomy class. Take a minute to collect your thoughts, see what you don't understand and ask your questions or form your comments and have a better shot at earning those participation points.

Now that you know the handy acronym of B.A.D., you have a much better chance of avoiding those dumb questions in class. So go through your list in your head before you ask your professor something. Make sure you don't know the answer, that you know this hasn't been discussed in the class before, that you really need the response in the now, and that it goes along with the discussion. You don't have to have some wondrous question that will stump the professor, but you should be mindful of your, your professor, and your classmates' time. Make sure your questions count and I promise you you'll have a better understanding of the material and more respect for it as well.

S
t
u
d
e
n
t

V
i
e
w

4 — Gratitude

not having any

"If you pick up a starving dog and make him prosperous, he will not bite you. This is the principal difference between a dog and a man."

—Mark Twain—
(Author/Humorist/Entrepreneur)

Professor Perspective:

All right. Raise your hand if you ever got an assignment back and you feel it wasn't appreciated enough by your teacher?

The sting can linger, can't it?

As an amusement park employee, I think, every day, I had to help a lost child find their parents. Sometimes, I'd have to take them to security so mommy or daddy could be paged. Most of the time, we were able to find the parents, and they were very gracious and thanked us.

I'm just kidding.

They never thanked us. The snatched the child up and started screaming at it.

I had a child wander away from his parents, squeeze through a fence and walk into my ride enclosure while the ride was in full operation. I pulled back on the brake, injured my shoulder and retrieved the child to return to grateful parents.

Just kidding! The father berated me, shoved on my injured shoulder, and then threatened to sue me—and I'm the one who saved the little snot's life after his parents stopped watching him.

I know what ingratitude looks like. It causes people to regret helping others. At the same time, it causes other people to think they deserve more and to become more ungrateful.

Ungrateful people find few allies.

In the university setting, students need all the allies they can find. Some day, they will graduate and apply for jobs that other people with similar degrees are also going to be applying for. The grateful student gets the support of teacher recommendations and word of mouth for opportunities from their peers. If there's one currency that students cannot afford to squander, it's help from others. No one wants to help ungrateful people. They might at first, but unless a person demonstrates gratitude, help will dwindle.

For example, I had a student email me at the beginning of a semester to tell me that he could not attend the first week because he was finishing another class at another university at that same time. Initially, I suggested the student not miss the first week or to take the class at a later date. He insisted that he had to take this class now, so I cut him a break and let him miss the first week. After that, every time an assignment came due, he asked for an extension on the deadlines.

I could see where this was going. He was going to avoid doing his work and then accuse me of not being more supportive as a teacher. I wanted to be able to say that I gave the student every break possible to help him succeed so that when he made this argument, he'd have no choice but to accept the consequences he created for himself. So, I allowed him to submit late. The first time he asked. He missed the extension. The second major assignment, he made the same request and missed that extension too.

Like I said, I knew the argument that was coming from him down the pipe, I even warned him about how what he was doing was going to affect his grades. He didn't believe me. The entire semester went this way, and I cut him many breaks that I gave no other student because no other ever needed the attention he did. At the end of the semester, on the final essay, he asked for another extension. I gave him a day. The student missed the extension and asked for another one. I was still in the process of grading the final papers and had ten days before I had to enter the final grades, so I asked him when he thought he could have the assignment to me. I let him pick his own reasonable deadline. Again, I knew where this was going.

Guess what? You'll never guess. He missed the deadline. He got the lowest grade in the class, even lower than people who stopped attending entirely.

When the class was over, it finally went where I knew it was going. He emailed me and politely asked if I would raise his grade. I refused, and his polite, begging facade fell. He started degrading me threatening that he was going to report me. I encouraged him to report me, and I explained that he wasn't going to like the outcome. He filed a complaint, and my supervisor came to me for a response. I supplied her with all of the emails I shared with him and all of the breaks I gave him. In response, my supervisor told my student she wasn't going to raise the grade. Then he went to the next supervisor up the chain, and nobody cared.

What he had failed to realize was that no one cared because he was ungrateful. He lost a teacher as an ally, a department as an ally, and an entire university as an ally. He could not appreciate that he had received support exceptions that went beyond what his own classmates required or requested, and he still lashed out over not getting better treatment.

It's easy for students to miss many of the help aids or breaks that a teacher gives behind the scenes.

I had a particular student who I felt needed a little encouragement. His history had been so filled with teachers pointing out his failures that I didn't think another low score was going to motivate him to discover a higher potential than he'd been allowed to realize before. So, I was a little more lenient with his points on one particular assignment, allowing him to earn a higher grade than I would have typically awarded.

Sometimes, you can tell when a student will learn nothing from another bad score. You can tell when a student is about to give up, and the best you can do to help is to cut that pupil a break and let him regroup. For one moment, the student can think, "Hey, maybe I'm not as stupid as I believed." That little self-affirmation can be the difference between students giving up on their studies and students feeling reinvigorated to prove their worth. Naturally, when I gave this one particular student a break and higher score than he earned, he was grateful.

Just kidding! The student started screaming about how low his grade was and I had to show him what he'd really earned, and I asked him which one he'd prefer.

Another student missed so many days of class that he qualified for an automatic F in the course. Out of compassion, I informed him that I would be willing to work with him if he didn't have any more absences. I explained, however, that the highest grade he could possibly earn was a C. His response was, "That won't work for me."

I replied with, "Will an F work for you, because that's what you've earned."

Something happens when students don't take the time to be grateful for what teachers (or others) do for them. They lose respect from the teacher, and the teacher loses interest in ever going out of the way to help that student again. Worse, it can add up until a teacher says, "I'll never offer that kind of help to *any* student again." And that's how immovable teachers begin to appear.

I love helping students succeed, but I don't love when a student lashes out after I did something kind for them.

The truth is, as a student, you can't always know what a teacher does. You are in the class because you don't know something about the topic, so you might not understand why you're not performing as well as you think you are. You might think you're performing the assignment or technique correctly, but you're actually doing it all wrong. You might not understand how you're misinterpreting instructions.

It can become a habit of students who put forth incorrect practices to say, "that is a bad teacher" when it is just as likely (moreso from my experience) that the student wasn't paying attention. For this, students can be blinded to showing gratitude when peers and professors take steps to help them understand it.

Believe me, there are messages that your instructors, even those who specialize in effective communication, misinterpret. If teachers can misinterpret them, students can misinterpret them. As a student, you might find yourself saying, "Then how am I supposed to know?"

It's simple. Learn how to say "thank you."

Every day, some students thank me after each class, and every semester, there are students who don't even bother to speak to me. It is interesting to note, that the students who thank me tend to be more aware of their responsibilities as students; more aware of my role as a teacher; more aware of the classroom as a community; more aware of seeking and accepting others' counsel; and more aware of how to do assignments than students who do not say "thank you."

Why?

Because students who learn to say "thank you" practice an attitude of being aware of their approaches and what others do for them. A student aware of what others do tends to participate and open up with more gracious behavior to their communities.

Occasionally, I will have students ask for the best advice I can give them for college, and I tell them to always thank their teachers. Simply thanking your professor puts you in a position to see that person as a human being, and to even engage them in conversation. It helps professors get to know you. It helps you practice speaking to them so you can feel more comfortable asking questions such as, "Why was my score so low," and then being open to the answer.

A classroom is not a selfish environment, but many students often act as though no other student exists. Learning to say *thank you* raises your awareness of the other people in the community.

This is the key to gratitude, and it's something every student should learn because it's how you expand your personal network.

In one of my graduate writing classes, I worked with a particular group of peers. One of them was a renowned author. When he presented his work to his peers, he started lashing out at them because he had never learned to take feedback. Having had enough, I finally told him, "You need to learn to shut up and listen." His response immediately became a tirade of, "How dare you tell me to shut up! Do you have any idea who I am? I could buy any one of you if I wanted." Seriously. He said this!

We, his learning community stopped talking to him. We stopped giving him feedback. No one wanted to work with him because he could not perform the simple act of acknowledging that we had sacrificed our time and energy to read his work and then give him feedback when we didn't have to. After he demonstrated he couldn't be grateful, we withdrew our support. We did not have to support him. This person may have been a New York Times bestselling author, but he was no writer, because writers listen to feedback. For the same reason, he was no scholar or student.

Teachers want to be your allies. However, nothing will turn them off to supporting a student faster than that student's ungrateful attitude, much like how this author-student turned off his own support system of peers and a professor.

See. Here's a secret: As teachers, we don't have to go the extra mile for you. All we have to do is lecture; provide opportunities for you to test the ideas and concepts presented in those lectures; and then calculate what we think the culmination of your investment in that work is worth when the time comes for us to pass judgment and award you points. Believe me, teachers don't have to be in your corner. We just have to be able to justify why we gave you the scores we gave you. Going the extra mile, bending over backwards, caring about your efforts? We don't have to do that for students who aren't grateful for our own efforts. There are others in the class who will appreciate the extra help we provide to help them succeed.

We don't even have to give you the best, personal comments to help you improve if we know those comments are going to fall on hard and unappreciative ears. We don't have to break down why you personally misunderstand information. We don't even have to answer your emails or take your phone calls with in-depth answers. We could answer everything with, "It's in the reading," or "borrow notes from someone." All we, as teachers, have to do is give you the information you need to earn points in the class, and if you can't interact with it, we'll be happy to deny you those points.

Or. . .

We can be your allies, and allies show gratitude to each other. For a teacher, it includes all the work I've just mentioned that we don't have to do. It includes work that goes beyond the classroom and that takes time from the teacher to give to a student (because the teacher cares). All a student has to do is learn how to say, "Thank you." That little act trains you to be aware of others. When you are aware of others, they go out of their ways to serve you when you need it most. Treat others like servants though, and they will exclude you from some of the greatest service you could use to succeed the most.

With my student who missed the first week of class and all of his deadlines, then proceeded to complain that I wasn't doing enough. Perhaps, if he had shown gratitude during the semester, he might have found an ally that might have said, "Okay, I've already posted grades, but let me see what options the university or department provides that I can consider to let you resubmit your work."

With all the ways that students can sabotage themselves, being ungrateful is the way to ensure teachers don't want to support you, and teachers have a lot of connections; write excellent letters of recommendation; and will remember you when opportunities arise. Nothing will ensure that they will withhold that from you more than being ungrateful.

Be ungrateful, and we will jump at the chance to write a letter that says, "My experience with this student has been one of ingratitude. If you were hiring someone to lick postage stamps, I would tell you to buy a dog instead."

Start learning to say "thank you," and you'll discover more ways to become aware of yourself and what others in your community have done for you. Students who learn to thank others, set themselves up not only to acknowledge what people do for them, but are more likely to serve others in a more giving capacity themselves. Serving others is how leaders rise through the ranks. Don't sabotage that potential for opportunity by denying yourself to understand how to serve. Learn to say "thank you," so you can learn how to serve, and hopefully you won't run into someone who hates you for that service like so many students hate teachers for their service.

Professors

View

Student Perspective:

If I had read this point when I was a sophomore in college, I think my reaction would have been something like this: Ungrateful? Well, what am I supposed to be grateful for? That I share a tiny room the size of a closet with a roommate that snores? That I'm living off a diet of Ramen and Taco Bell? That I'm always tired and never have any free time to myself?

As you can see, it's very difficult to see what exactly there is as a student to be grateful for. So, what would it really mean to be ungrateful? I think that's where the problem lies. Students are so focused on what they don't have, or what they're currently suffering through, that they don't even spend a half second to be grateful for what they do have. This ends up morphing into something you wouldn't expect most poor starving students who are barely scraping by to have: entitlement.

Now I'm not talking about the Blair Waldorf "I deserve to go to Yale because I'm rich and pretty and deserve it" type of entitlement, but rather one that stems from exhaustion, anger, and a craving for recognition. Don't get me wrong, being a student is one of the hardest and (in the moment) most unfulfilling roles. However, because there is no immediate gratification from school assignments like those that can come from a normal job or task, it can cause students to seek it out in other places.

For example, if I pulled an all-nighter for my current job, I am almost positive that not only would I receive high praise and gratitude from my boss, but things would run smoother in my position. I might even get a raise or gift card out of it. However, if I did the same thing as a student, all that I would get out of it is (hopefully) a better score on my test. The sad truth is, when you're a student you're doing everything for yourself with no real tangible reward other than that illusionary diploma fluttering over your head. This is what causes that sense of entitlement.

Sometimes it comes in forms of "I should definitely get an extension on this paper. It's unfair, I put in so much hard work!" Or, "This is ridiculous for them to expect this of me! Don't they see how busy I am?" And, lastly, my personal favorite, "How dare they grade me so hard on this test! I deserved way higher than that!"

If any of these phrases sound at all familiar to you, then you have probably suffered from a case of student entitlement sometime in your past. And that is okay. We all do it. Student life is tough. Sometimes all we need is to feel like we deserve a bit of a break.

One of my favorite examples of student entitlement came in my last semester of school. I had that senior apathy, and I was ready to be *done*. I had five different essays to write and three practical tests all in the span of a week.

One of these papers was an absolute monster at 21 pages long. Because of the length of the assignment, some of those 21 pages were lacking in my usual substance and I couldn't find it in myself to care. I had other, shorter essays that needed my focus. However, a dear friend of mine, (we'll call him Luke) like a saint, agreed to read through and edit all of my essays. We spent hours editing and revising late into the night, and he helped me make that monster of a paper into something presentable.

Cue three weeks later. We're hanging out playing video games at his apartment, and he asks how I did on my finals. I pulled up my grades and told him how, on that big whopper of a paper that he helped me with, I got an 83%. Immediately, Luke launched into a tirade that went something along the lines of this: "How dare they! You poured your heart and soul into this essay! You deserved a way better score and—

I interrupted him to say, "Luke, you and I both know that an 83% was generous, and frankly more than I deserved." Luke went quiet, staring down at the video game controller in his lap and then said, "Well—yeah—but I figured someone needed to fight for you."

Besides being absolutely hilarious, Luke spoke the truth. We as students are looking for someone to fight for us. And more often than not, that person is ourselves, hence the entitlement. But sometimes, we can choose the wrong people to fight against.

It's the hard truth that, in actuality, we are very lucky to be students. School is not only difficult, but it's expensive and time-consuming. Despite this, it leads to edifying independence and self-improvement that are hard-won skills. However, as we are on this grueling journey to achieve our degrees and gain all of the good things that come from getting an education, it can be easy to point our fingers at the hard things in our lives. This can lead to taking advantage of professors, other students, and even the college as a whole, and it can lead to coming up with excuses for not trying as hard.

I remember one day, after spending hours studying, I was finally preparing for bed and talking to my roommate about our days. After complaining for a bit, I asked her about the essay she had due that evening. She shrugged and told me she hadn't started on it yet. I quickly looked at the clock in a panic. She had an hour left to write an entire essay! She just shrugged and told me she had emailed the professor seeking an extension, and he had approved it.

This absolutely blew me away that one, her professor would just approve an extension that early (I had to practically beg for an extension when my grandfather passed away); and two, that she hadn't even tried at all to submit the essay at the normal due date! Now, this is not to throw my friend under the bus. I did many similar things like this as well, such as not finishing a presentation on the due date because I knew that there were two presentation days. I just made sure to not present on the first day. We all do things like this because we feel that we, as students, deserve a bit of clemency, or a bit of a break. However, this ungratefulness will get you nowhere. Sometimes you will get away with it, like my friend did.

However, that soon leads into a ruthless habit of just expecting things to go your way with a laziness that will eventually fall into a rude awakening. One day you'll run into a professor or a class or an assignment that you can't work your way around, and no amount of angry words (like the ones from my friend Luke) will change anything about getting the grade you deserve.

So, be grateful for what you do have, and the opportunities given to you. You have a chance to learn and be surrounded by interesting minds in the form of your fellow students and your professors. Jump at the chance to try new things and discover more about yourself, and you won't be caught in a river of self entitlement that leads to nowhere.

5 — Wrong Goals
recognizing you're adults

"One of the greatest struggles of becoming an adult is figuring out what you want to do and what makes you happy. The courageous thing is to stick with it and see it through and see if you were correct."

—Kristen Stewart—
(Actor)

Professor Perspective:

Hollywood would have you believe that when a locomotive falls off its tracks a mile away from where you're crossing, you better run, because that derailed behemoth is now going to chaotically chase you for five more miles. All the while it will be laughing maniacally at your feeble attempt to flee.

The reality is, that train is not designed to travel on anything other than rails. So, if it falls off the tracks, it will plant and anchor itself. If it moves at all after that, it will be at a snail's pace while the rest of the train slowly folds in on itself behind the engine. It is a slow, destructive process that requires a lot of work, machinery, and hands to reset the engine in its rails.

The reason I bring this up is because this is quite similar to how too many university students derail their own studies.

Students who do not set their own desired paths to reach their learning goals are highly likely to give up, especially when their education is being directed by what another person wants them to study. Students who derail will anchor themselves where they fall and require a lot of support to get moving again. This can include finding, or helping others to find, the momentum to start studying again.

There is a brick wall that every student without goals, without preparation, without personalizing their learning desires will hit if they don't establish and visualize their own path to earning a degree. Many students can come into college, expecting it to be a we'll-see-what-happens environment, only to find their studies screeching to an emotionally devastating halt.

Part of the reason for this is because secondary education has trained students into a pattern of "you take the classes we give you. If you happen to get one you want, then count yourself lucky." This is a pattern where an individual is forced to learn according to someone else's learning agenda. Yet, that is not how higher education works.

Higher education says that you can study what you want, all you have to do is plan ahead and stick that plan through.

University students who look at the semester in front of them, but not at the full tour, neglect to identify what that journey is and where it will take them. When a student looks at the entire university venture, they can understand its different legs (semesters, classes, etc.), and they can feel the progression. They learn to establish an ownership and understanding of how their individuality can personally contribute to their potential communities.

Students who do not do this will too often hit brick walls and realize that, rather than directing their own educational journey, someone else has been directing it. We don't discover where we want to go though when we're following someone else's path.

What do I mean by following another person's path? Any time that you are taking courses that someone else desires to take, or vicariously desires to take through you, that is someone else's path. Any time you are studying because that's what someone else wants, that is not your path (unless you actually want it too). Your learning path is what you want to study. You might have to discover what you want though, and it will still demand work and sacrifice.

Following another person's goals sabotages our own and numbs our desire to even seek our own paths. Worse, not finishing someone else's path can make you feel like a failure and less likely to believe you can complete your own—because you never learned the joy of exploring your own. Failing on a another person's path can make you feel like you can't succeed on yours.

See, here's something about the journey of learning that can help any student if they just allow themselves to discover it: Human brains enjoy being active. A brain that discovers its own energy and what it wants to do, hungers to learn more and to move forward. That is the magic of learning. Yet, when another person pushes you to make your brain seek what their brain hungers, then your own brain starves.

It's easy for our peers and people we respect to forget this. While their brains may thrive upon topics that energize them, they can forget that those same topics might not energize our minds. While my friend may thrive in quantum philosophy, my brain would be happy to take an F in that class because it just doesn't care.

This is the basis for the biggest complaints that I've heard from students with no energy before they dropped out of college.

One of the biggest ways you can sabotage yourself as a student is to go to college for the sole purpose of making someone else's brain happy. The university journey is supposed to be yours. Afterall, only you will ever live with your brain.

Students who lay the path for their own desired education take joy in discovery along the way.

So, how do you combat becoming trapped into someone else's plan that you don't really want to take?

There's a solution, and it's simple: You are adults. That's something college students forget. As university students, you are adults surrounded by other adults, and you are all free to choose to be who you want to be, to sign up for classes you want to; to choose a major you enjoy; to take pride in what others have inhibited before. When you realize this and you plan your own path, you will find that learning is a drug. Your brain will want more. It's difficult to believe though when you might come from a background of, "You take the classes we give you and shut up."

That, of course, is not higher learning philosophy.

Okay, so what if you don't know what direction you want to go? Start by taking a university catalog and perusing through the degrees it offers. Read the course descriptions. When you start to find a cluster of classes in a field that you find tantalizes your brain, that's a clue that you're on the right track of what empowers you. Some universities have means to build your own degree. Some offer integrated degrees. I know many people with degrees that they designed with help from their advisers and universities.

Many students don't realize that one of the purposes of general eds is to help you discover disciplines of study that you might not realize you like. This is another way you can discover what interests you: Test the general ed courses for yourself.

Be adults. Study what approaches other students have taken. You have an adviser, but keep in mind that this isn't your adviser's journey either. I've known many advisers who have steered students wrong. I know one student whose adviser didn't know what she was doing and kept the student she was supposed to represent from graduating. It wasn't until the student broke ties with the individual adviser that the student realized she could have graduated years earlier. The adviser had been preventing the student from taking one class the student needed to complete her diploma requirements. The adviser even convinced the student to switch majors into a field that the adviser thought the student should seek. By doing so, the adviser denied the student her own interests and paused her graduation and career.

You're adults. Tap into your freedom. Set your own journey.

Children don't get to define their own journeys. They must conform to many powers of influence, but adults get to choose for themselves.

Does it mean you won't have to take classes or have discussions that you're not interested in? No, but It's a lot easier to sit through a class on a topic that you don't like when you're allowed to discover how it relates to the topic that you *do* care about. If you define your full journey, you'll see how less-intriguing discussions can enhance the ones you are interested in, and that is what makes an individual student's own educational, adventurous path easier to follow and to keep following.

Student Perspective:

College is kind of a weird concept when you think about it. You take a bunch of kids who just came out of a high school where the most important thing that happened was that their football team almost made it to state. Then, you expect those same students to care and focus in a highly competitive intellectual environment. Truth is, there is a reason that people call us college kids. Despite legally being considered adults once you reach the ripe, old age of eighteen, the sad truth is many of us don't fully grasp that. The change from high school kid to college kid is so immediate that it's hard to feel different. However, retaining the same mindset from high school is one of the fatal mistakes a new student can make.

In order to help you understand the big difference between college-level and high school-level, I would like to share a high-school experience, not a college one. I grew up in a town of about seven thousand people, all together. Everyone knew everyone, and that was just the way of things.

In one of my classes, we had a big assignment coming up where we presented on a book that we had just read. I loved this course, and I loved this teacher, so I was looking forward to it. She had laid out several days that were just presentation time. I had finished reading the book ages ago and was nearly done with my report. I just needed a couple more slides left for my presentation. However, I wasn't in a panic, I would just present on day two. Other people would volunteer day one; I could just present day two; and no one would be the wiser. At least that's what I thought. When I got to class that first day, my beloved teacher announced that she would be drawing the presenters at random. I felt my heart drop out of my chest. Yes, there was a slim chance I would be asked to speak but a chance nonetheless and I was not ready.

As the first poor presenter began, I whipped out my phone under the desk and pleaded for aid from the only person that had the capacity to help me in my time of need—my mother.

Luckily, this class was my last one of the day, so I just begged her to pull me out early, that I would come home and complete the assignment and help her make dinner. My blessed mother asked next to no questions, pulled me out of class, and took me home where I promptly finished the assignment.

The next day I found out my name had been pulled immediately after I left class, and that this beloved teacher had declared I would go first today. As I stood up to read my (thankfully) completed presentation my teacher called out, "I hope you're ready Miss Kunzler, because your sweet mother can't save you this time!"

Despite the humor of the situation, my teacher was correct that my "sweet mother" would not always be there to save me in my time of need. That is the difference between college and high school, the difference between being an adult and being a teenager. The things we depend on, such as the people that will help us and lift us up when we fall, aren't there anymore—Or, at least, not in the same capacity.

In College, you are responsible for yourself. You are accountable for not finishing an assignment, or for coming in late, or getting a failing grade. Your sweet mothers won't be there to bail you out of a situation you weren't ready for. That is one thing that is a very rude awakening to experience, especially if you always had people helping and encouraging you right before you started college. You won't have a helpful little angel on your shoulder showing you where to buy cheap books and where each class is. It's just going to be you. Welcome to adulthood my friends.

So how exactly do students not act like they're adults? It's not like you can just raise your hand and go, "Sorry professor, I didn't turn this in because my mom didn't remind me, and I wanted to go to a party last night." No, forgetting you're an adult can be a lot more subtle than that, and more damaging. It's all about not setting goals.

In high school, for the most part, you could float by. I'm not saying high school wasn't hard, but it had different expectations. You got good grades so you could get into a good college. You didn't stay out too late because your parents wouldn't let you. You ate well because that's what was given to you. Being an adult, however? Whole different ball park. All of that falls on you. You need to get good grades because you want good grades. You don't stay out too late because you have the self-discipline to balance school and a social life. You eat well because when you first ate a meal of just fruit gushers and hot pockets you got sick, and now you care about yourself enough to not get scurvy.

So, now that it has become super obvious that you're on your own in college and responsible for your individual success, how do you start acting like an adult? You start by making your own goals. Too many students start college with the fly-by-the-seat-of-your-pants type of attitude. They think that they can just do the song and dance and get by. However, when you're in charge of yourself you have to put in a little bit more effort than that—by making goals, and I don't mean the same ones will apply for everyone.

We all learn differently, so the same thing that works for one student won't work for you. The first step is understanding who you are as a student. Your student-identity is how you study, how you learn, how you think, how you unwind, and what you need to do to most likely succeed. For some students this is spending hours in the library poring over your notes. For others, it's getting a big study session together. And for some, it's de-stressing with video games. For me, it was doing headstands while I memorized facts. Your method is your method, and your goals are your goals. That's the beauty of being responsible for yourself. It's all you, but the good thing is that you are the person who knows you best.

So, how do you set goals? For some people, making a planner is the way to do it. The best way for them to keep on top of all of their responsibilities is writing it down. I also know of others who take a weekly meeting with themselves to prepare for their week by talking it out. I know others that can keep it somehow successfully all in their heads. So, set your attainable goals in the way that works for you and make the next step: following through.

So many of my fellow students have grand plans. They figure out that they're on their own and they are determined to ace it. However, when it comes to the issue of actually following through with your meticulous scheduling and ideas, that is where it becomes daunting.

It's easy to wish for the days of being a teenager, where you had support and planned-out activities, where you couldn't slip into your own folly and time-wasting leisure as easily. However, those days are gone. Instead, welcome to the days of self-discipline. You can't use excuses because no one is there to hear them but yourself. So, set your plan, carry it out, and expect it to fail in the beginning. College is the time of growth and trial and error. Don't be afraid if you struggle to make the leap into self-sufficiency. It doesn't come naturally. Give yourself time, find what works and stick with it.

This section might feel a bit preachy, and I get that. I don't want to be talking down to you, that is definitely not my intention. I have been in your shoes though, and recently. However, if you want to be a successful student that doesn't go crying home to mom at every step, you'll learn how to understand yourself and take accountability. Get to like yourself for your success and also like yourself for how you deal with your failures. If you can do this, you will be well on your way to being a successful and independent student.

Student

View

6 — Taking Notes

| *lying to yourself* |

"As a painter, taking photos is a form of shorthand."

—Wanda Koop—
(Artist)

Professor Perspective:

Truth: Talking about taking notes is boring. Taking notes is boring. There is probably more joy to be had in drinking your bald professor's hair tonic (you know who I'm talking about).

What's important though is understanding you can't take note-taking for granted. It's your lifeline to higher grades, especially in difficult classes. This cannot be emphasized enough. You can't expect effective note-taking to just turn on when you find yourself in those situations where you need them most— because you won't know how, although you might think you do.

Everyone thinks they know how to take good notes though, and it often causes us not to consider how to make them better and more helpful. When it comes to taking notes, either you keep accurate records, or you take incomplete ones. Notes that don't effectively help you recall information are incomplete, even dishonest. No, you didn't cheat because of how you wrote them down. They're simply incomplete, and you can't honestly recall the information you need. They're dishonest because you, who knows how to speak to yourself

Professor Wise

better than anyone else, did not speak to yourself through your own notes in a way to help you remember what you needed to.

So, just for a moment, forget your current, note-taking approaches. Start with a clean slate. Forget notes you've taken, forget what anyone's ever told you about taking notes. Just erase the board on the topic of taking notes entirely. Then every time you find yourself in a discussion on note-taking, wipe the board clean again because that opens you up to make your notes stronger. You open yourself to new information and new approaches to record information that helps you get higher grades.

Okay, why?

Regardless of your note-taking approaches, your notes are the heartbeat of your classes, more than the text book, more than the teacher. They are more accessible to you. They are just for you.

You are going to hear many people say that you should or shouldn't do something in the way that you take notes. If your notes are helping you remember and organize important information, those notes are working. And if people say you should not use that kind of note-taking approach, those people are wrong. However, that doesn't mean you can't learn to communicate with yourself better and tweak your techniques to make your notes better.

Taking notes is personal, and what people forget is that there's no one-size-fits-all note-taking system that works for every person, in every discipline, in every style learning. Educators and researchers have often spent so much time investigating the results of immediate compiled notes, that they have often neglected to acknowledge behavioral approaches in note-taking with students.

I told you this topic is boring. Boooooooring!

Still, notes are the best way to earning higher grades. So, start with a clean slate regarding what you know about note-taking.

Understand that note-taking is a conversation where you translate what others are saying to yourself. The notes are not for your teacher, not for the authors of your books. They are for you. If you don't speak to yourself in a way that you understand, how can you possibly expect your teacher to do it through you as the translator? When taking notes, you are your own translator to other people's ideas.

I am not going to tell you that your note-taking approaches are bad. You will run into plenty of people who will be happy to do that without my help.

Instead, I'm going to show you how you can put yourself into a better position to translate information more completely, based upon the environment you may find yourself in.

Just as putting words on paper is a small part of the writing process, so too is writing notes down only a small part of note-taking. The biggest and most helpful parts of keeping notes come from getting to know your various, learning environments where you will need to record information. Knowing your classroom helps you to identify the tools you will need to supplement your translation approaches.

Here is how we can prepare ourselves:

1. Get to know your environment and tools to work in it.
2. Get to know people in your environment.
3. Take part in your environment.
4. Record the environment.
5. Question within the environment.

1. Get to know your environment and tools to work in it:

You cannot write as fast as a person speaks. Even skilled court reporters with keyboards that can abbreviate entire sets of keystrokes cannot record words as fast as witnesses spew them out. Judges often have to tell witnesses to speak slowly. So, if you are a slow writer, as everyone is, why would you enter a fast-speaking lecture with the slowest modern ways of recording information—a pen and paper, or even a laptop—and expect to capture all the information you need to recall? You need more. Knowing what kind of environment that you are going into can help you identify the right tools to begin with.

I'm not saying you should ever write down every word someone says, but good notes help you recall them.

For instance, a recording device or app will allow you to revisit the lecture. I know it can be boring to listen to a professor drone on more than once, but recording devices can allow you to bookmark complicated discussions. Imagine taking notes during a confusing concept and being able to look at the time stamp of your recording. You know right where in your lecture to revisit that information later if you need to. Most recording apps and devices allow the ability to bookmark directly to discussions you want to revisit.

Whaf if the environment you're taking notes in is a book?

In a class with heavy definition regurgitation, despite what people say, highlighting has been an effective tool for many students to help locate definitions in a textbook quickly, but it might not be so great at providing trigger words to help you remember the definition. I've had a long line of professors try to convince me that highlighting didn't work, yet I can point to several classes where it helped me earn the highest possible grade. I'm not alone in this either.

So, maybe you identify that you need to take a highlighter to make definitions stand out, and a pencil so you can write notes in the margins. However, maybe you've learned that it's easy to lose notes in a margin when those margins have too many notes, or your book has too many highlighted markings.

Some people will say that if you write more notes than the actual passage of a piece of text you are reading, you have written too much. Yet, what if that small passage alludes to a larger idea where expanding the picture to yourself allows you to connect dots and identify relationships to similar ideas? Could a denser note to yourself help? Absolutely! If you understand the notes, that's an effective note system. Who has the right to tell you what you shouldn't do in your notes, if you find your notes work for you?

So, maybe the tools you identify to take notes in a book include highlighter, pencil, and a separate notebook. What's important here is that you pick the tools that work for you. I know one student who reads his chapters out loud so he can hear the words, and he records himself as though it were a lecture, and he'll even take notes while listening to his recordings.

That might seem overkill for a simple information, but it helped him earn an A in a highly demanding and stressful class.

2. Identify the people in the environment:

Straight up, get to know your classmates. Move around the class. Watch how others take notes. Learn who takes good ones, so you can ask them for details you might have missed in your own, especially if you should be absent from a lecture. You might also be helping them to refocus themselves in their own notes. Knowing someone else can give you access to what you missed.

Identifying the people in your environment helps to provide you with allies and insight on the topics discussed in class.

3. Take part in the environment:

For as much as good note-taking can help students understand a concept, if the teacher provides an opportunity to practice that concept then take it. Don't just get involved with that activity, leave yourself a note about how you got involved. It will help you remember the concept and the exercise. Doing is mnemonic. I've conducted activities in classes where I've had students forget we did them. Later, they may come up to question a particular concept, and I point back to the activity. Students who participate in these activities often erupt with "oh yeah!" when I remind them of it. Even if you think the activity is stupid, taking part in that *stupid* activity helps you remember more than if you didn't take part in that *stupid* activity.

Participating in your environment is a form of interactive note-taking. You can record your activity in the event to trigger the concepts it represented and the experiences that you had while taking part.

4. Record the Environment:

Put actual words on paper that may remind you of something that happened in the environment.

When I was a student, I recorded a time when someone belched in class, and the students erupted in laughter. It also happened to be a day that my professor said I was absent. I looked to my notes, and I said, "No, it was the day that Tim belched in class when we were talking about this." Then my professor said, "Oh yeah."

Record events in the the environment. Those events can trigger memories. You never know what details will help you recall conversations or context (or protect your attendance record).

5. Question within the environment:

Revisit your notes after the note-taking session. Read them while they're fresh. Study them between classes, but do so quickly to help you identify concepts you may have missed or misunderstood, and that will allow you to write down follow-up questions, while they're fresh in your mind (or you forget them).

After the note-taking session, if you have gaps in your notes, ask others in your environment (teacher, fellow students you got to know who take good notes). Ask them face-to-face to clarify information you put to paper, and then write those comments down as well. Email others, set up study groups. For the record, people do not share notes enough in study groups. When you have a group of several people sharing notes, you can clarify information, you can discover confusing concepts so you can collectively ask the teacher later about them later.

Asking follow-up questions provides opportunity to revisit the topic and to commit information to memory even further.

In my experience and observations, note-taking isn't about right or wrong. It's about being honest with the way you speak to yourself. If you have gaps in your translations, it's not an honest nor accurate translation. However, if you adopt a system that allows you to fill in those gaps by bringing the right tools to your environment; knowing your environment and the people within it; and then asking follow-up note-taking questions, you can add to your personal records. That is what makes for effective note-taking. That leads to higher grades.

Note-taking is not just about technique. It's about habit and behavior, but we easily, and too often, focus on the technique over the habit and behavior.

If you understand your notes, and they're helping you recall the information that you need to succeed, then those notes are working, despite what others may try to argue.

It's when you start accepting that it's normal to maintain incomplete and dishonest notes to yourself that you sabotage your class points and ability to fully understand your topic. Incomplete (dishonest) notes translate to lower grades. Know your environment, the people in it, use them with your tools to fill in the gaps. It might be more work, but you'll feel rewarded—even though it is *boring*.

Student Perspective:

In my time as a student, I lied to myself—a lot. Maybe not the best thing to do but when your life is chaotic, as a student's always is, you end up telling a lot of lies to yourself. Such as: "I'll be fine going to this party, I'll still get to that essay I need to finish, no problem," or "that was definitely my best work. I'm going to get a great grade on it," or my personal favorite: "I don't need to study that hard for that test. It's going to be a breeze!"

Whether it be procrastination, blind optimism, or a last ditch resort to make yourself feel better, you're going to lie to yourself at some point through college. However, the more often this happens, the more disastrous it becomes on your well-being as a student. You can't live in delusion forever. Eventually, reality will come crashing down. Although we all use these little lies to ourselves to get through hard classes or moments, there are times when you should most certainly not be lying to yourself. One of those is in your very own note-taking.

You might be asking, "How do I lie to myself in note-taking?" There are quite a few ways, but one of them leads back to a point I've discussed in previous sections: Knowing Yourself. This may seem like the most basic piece of advice. After all, college is a place to find and know yourself, but many people miss this mark. When I say "know yourself," I mean know how you study best and how you understand things. Time and again, I see people taking notes—because that's how they feel they should take them, or because that's the effort they want to put in. However, it doesn't work that way. Let me tell you a story about my brother, we'll call him John.

John loves everything new technology. He has the newest computer, the newest sound system, and could debate for hours about the differences between Apple and Samsung and which one you should choose. For the sake of not offending anyone, I will leave his very passionate opinion on that matter out of this. It shouldn't come as a surprise that, when I entered college, John had all of these opinions about what type of computer

Student V, i, e, w

would be best for me school-wise. John's own computer was a touchscreen that could flip into a tablet, and he convinced me of all the ways that a computer like his would be beneficial for my note-taking in class.

"Not only can you use it as a keyboard, Elyse, but you'll also be able to use it like a pen and paper, and then you can transfer these notes to a normal computer document! You'll love it, I promise!"

John's enthusiasm had me sold. I got a computer similar to his that worked with my budget and needs, and I was excited to try out all of the new fangled options in class. Except, it didn't work like that at all. After the first couple of days of trying to use my computer in the ways John had shown me, I came to the conclusion that I was lying to myself. I wasn't like John. I wasn't the type to take notes that way, and it was showing.

So, you want to know what I used my whole glorious college career to take notes? A nice Pilot G-2 0.7mm pen and a simple notebook. This isn't an ad. I'm just passionate about this pen brand, I swear. That's all I used. That's how Elyse Kunzler takes notes. That works for me. Initially, I was lying to myself by trying to take notes how I thought I should be taking notes, like John.

Don't make my mistake. Find what works for you when you're note-taking. For some students, it's typing away on their laptops. For others, it's using a normal pen and paper, while some people use fancy note-taking programs or other artistic ways. Don't feel like you need to note-take a certain way to succeed in class. Scrawled scribbles that only you understand can be just as effective as a fancy PowerPoint presentation, if that's the way that you best learn. Don't underestimate your own abilities in the face of what you might perceive to be better.

Another way of lying to yourself in your notes is by what you actually include in them or leave out. For some people, when a professor is discussing something, you may think, "Oh, that's a really easy concept," or "oh, I won't forget that," and then you just leave it out of your notes. In the heat of the moment, it may seem ludicrous that you would ever forget that important bit of information. Yet, no matter how memorable the information is, you're going to be learning a lot of things. Then, when it's the final hour, and you're desperately searching through your notes for that one piece of information that fled your mind. You'll be at a loss for what exactly you forgot to put in your notes.

"Oh, what did Professor Harward say? I know it was important and about binomials."

Another way students lie to themselves, that I've seen and experienced, is thinking you're smarter than you are in your own notes. That's doing things like just writing one or two words and being confident that you'll remember what you were writing about. We can see this when we might find ourselves writing down the entire scientific definition of words. I did this a couple of times where I would be looking for definitions, find one in my notes, and then be very disappointed in myself as I had written down the definition but not in a way that I understood it. Then I would have to do some additional work googling and researching to understand a topic that I could have, and should have, understood in class.

Trust me though, I get it. I'm a PowerPoint note-taker. What this kind of note-taking is, is writing down basically word-for-word what is in your professor's PowerPoints. However, this becomes a problem when one of your professors conveniently doesn't use PowerPoints and is more of a lecturer. Despite your professor's teaching style, one of the best and most important things to learn as a student is how to note-take in all classes and to not lie to yourself when you do it. It comes down to a few simple skills. The first is understanding the main topic.

On my notes, I would boil down the lecture of the day to roughly one topic. For a literature class, perhaps we are talking about one genre or book. For a math class, you might be learning one type of algorithm or theory. Whatever it is, for the most part, you'll be aware of what your topic is for that day. Perfect. Next step is identifying the sub-topics.

Most professors will break down this topic into mini-lessons or speaking points. Let's say, for example, that we're in a literature class and we're talking about gothic literature (don't worry. You won't have a quiz on this after). Your professor's subtopics might be something like: Women in gothic literature, the moral dilemma in gothic literature, and the effects of the sublime in gothic literature. Each of those will be your professor's main speaking points.

A perfect way to formulate your notes for the day is by filing them into these broader topics of the one main focus. For instance, you might have an entire page that has all of your notes concerning women in gothic literature. You'll have bullet points on Mary Shelley and Ann Radcliffe, and then you might have some subsections or notes if your professor goes a little off topic or has information you know is critical to your grade. This is just a form of rough note-taking. You should definitely add your own spin and see what works for you, but having this rough idea of note-taking will help you best utilize it.

When you're in a stressful class where the professor is talking too fast, or too slowly, or talking too complicated, take a deep breath. Focus on where your strengths lie in note-taking.

Do you use fancy programs? A computer? Pen and Paper? Whatever it is, pick up your chosen weapon. Next, think of the important parts of what your professor is saying and put them down in a way that you will best understand them. Will you really understand that the scrawled word "lake" next to your notes on the sublime will remind you of that one specific painting your professor brought up? If not, maybe be a bit more clear in your writing. Next, make sure that you organize your notes in a way that will be helpful to you. There's no use in having notes if you're not going to use them. Once you've done these steps, and are confident in your note-taking, you are ready to go. So, stop lying to yourself in your notes and utilize them to serve you.

Student

View

7 — Lying

to others

"I do not mind lying, but I hate inaccuracy."

—Samuel Butler—
(Critic and Author)

Professor Perspective:

I usually like my teachers, but there was one in particular I did not respect. He was nice to everyone except me, and I never understood why. Everyone got ten minutes to do their presentations. When it came time to give mine, he interrupted me one minute in and told me I had two minutes, which threw off my entire plan. It upset the class, some complained to the department about his treatment of me, but he didn't care.

One of my classmates took her essay in to him to get his feedback before it was due, and he told her that in its current condition, it would earn a B. He informed her that if she made changes that they discussed in their meeting, it would earn an A. She made the changes, and he gave her a C-. He played dirty tricks that unfairly affected his students' grades.

I definitely didn't like being in his class, and I learned that giving my all would never be enough because, for whatever reason, he chose to not like me. We never argued, I came from a school that, unlike today, we treated our professors with respect. You never heard a student lash out at a teacher. Still, he hated me.

So, when we had an essay due on a Friday, I didn't have a lot of sincere investment. I didn't want to fail the class, but I knew what I knew—he sucked. I didn't really put my all into my 12-page essay because I knew the energy wouldn't be worth it. When it got down to the wire, I had 11 pages, and I wasn't done. I had no intention of finishing. I was tired. I had an early class in four hours, and I knew getting that last page out would take away from needed sleep.

I typed to the end of page 11 and stopped. I stapled all the typed pages together, plus a blank one at the end of the assignment. Then, I carefully tore off the final, blank page so there was paper stuck under the staple to appear that the sheet had been torn off somehow, and I turned the assignment in. I'd hoped he'd think it was an unfortunate accident.

After I turned it in, later that day, I wrote the last page.

The professor emailed me on Saturday and informed me that I was missing a page and wondered if I was aware that it might have torn off. To which I responded, "Oh my gosh, no! Here is my full essay," and I emailed it back. Got an A-.

The sad thing is that I was actually proud of that A-.

But why? To answer that, let me switch gears to the teacher role and then we'll come back.

As teachers, we have a faculty meeting every year before school starts. We get instruction from various departments, and, for several years, one of those departments opened every meeting with a promise that went like this: "We promise not to believe anything your students say about you, if you promise not to believe anything your students say about us."

Now, to some, this may seem like a negative and cynical outlook that establishes the attitudes that professors will enter the school year with when regarding student behavior. I can see why it would be easy to believe that.

However, it pains me to say that I have never met more dishonest people in my life than students. And the need for department heads and teachers to have to even make statements such as these testifies to the abundance that we see of students lying to us across the college campus. Now, it doesn't bother me with the inventive ways that students try to manipulate me. What bothers me is that students think I'm so dumb, and that I've never seen it before.

I've had simple lies: The two students who emailed me and said they were in a car accident, even brought a doctor's note stating that they needed recovery time, is a favorite of mine. I remember walking behind one of them on our way towards our next class and watching her race through crosswalks and down hallways. The second she hit the threshold to our classroom, she suddenly bent forward, limped, put her hand on her back. When I asked her how they were doing, she said, "Oh, the pain is still lingering." She wasn't aware that I'd already seen her dodging people in the hallways and running across the street. Nor was she aware that the public pictures and videos, which she and her classmate posted on social media during the time they were both "recovering" at the hospital, showed them both playing at Disneyland instead. Did I tell them that I knew they were lying? No, but I also never gave them any leniency or extra effort on my part.

See, there are just certain understandings that come with being a teacher that most people don't fully appreciate. For instance, professors are well aware that all grandparents die on final exam day. So, we teachers have to all prepare for that funeral rush at the end of the semester. Some students' grandparents are lucky enough to have superpowers that allow them to resurrect afterwards, which permits them to die two or three more times that semester, usually on days when other tests and assignments are due.

There's always a car accident when it's time to turn in essays in class where you meet face-to-face. When those same essays are due in an online class, I promise everyone's neighbor will be digging in the backyard and cutting your buried Internet cable. Then it will take at least three...teen... thirteen day...weeks before the cable company can get to it, but—"hey—I can still find a way to email you to say I can't submit my work online."

As a teacher, you know that when you read end-of-semester evaluations that students write, there will always be one student who thinks lying about you will get you fired, when what it really shows is that the student wasn't paying attention in class.

The reality is, university work is hard, and students can often feel overwhelmed and alone. When we feel that combination, we can be tempted to believe we truly are running solo. If we add in experiencing a history of having professors who have no-tolerance policies; who see no exceptions to any rules; who don't give students a reason to trust them, it's very easy to feel that being dishonest is the only way to give yourself that little bit of breathing room to let you put the finishing touches on an assignment.

I was never a perfectionist as a student, but I wanted my work to be done. So, I understand that some students just need extra study time. Some students have test anxiety. Some students are perfectionists. Some students just need thirty more minutes to catch their breaths.

Because of feeling alone, overwhelmed, or distrusting that a teacher will support you, it can be easy for a student to be tempted to buy that breathing room by presenting their professor a scenario-excuse that a normal, compassionate person wouldn't argue with.

I've found there's three ways teachers typically react when a student needs more time to complete an assignment. The first one allows you more time. The second says "Give me what you have, and you can resubmit it later for a higher grade." The third says, "No. Absolutely not. I refuse to budge for whatever reason that I've developed to not budge."

It's that teacher who says "no" that scares students into asking themselves: "What if this other teacher also says 'no'?" That fear can drive the student to contemplate a surefire way to convince any of those teachers to say "yes." Who can argue with a dying grandma? Just ask Johny Fairplay from *Survivor*.

This is even more complicated when we throw another factor in. Teachers want to support students (good teachers do)—but teachers, despite what students may think—are ultimately bound by curriculum and expectations that are governed by board and accreditation committees. These actually say: "Degrees that come from that university are valid." That's where we're likely to run into teachers who will say, "If you ever need anything, let me know," but then when you ask them, they may have to say, "Oof! That particular reason doesn't fall into a category that I can justify excusing." So, students can become afraid that a teacher who is supportive, may still say "no" to a request.

So, where does that put students when they might need that extra breathing room?

It puts them in a position to ask honestly.

See, teachers have been around this a long time. They've done this whole studying-at-a-university thing themselves. They know the sound of dishonesty, but if they went around failing every student for every lie they told a teacher to get a piece of breathing room, we'd have empty universities. Really, in many ways, it is an environment that outdated and overly strict pedagogy has enabled. In reality, we typically don't call students out for little, white lies.

Regardless, teachers remember dishonest students.

Because teachers' hands are sometimes tied from awarding leniencies at times, it can make a student feel good when they were able to find a way to get some breathing room to allow them to finish an assignment. Can we say that getting breathing room is something to be ashamed of? If it's taken dishonestly, sure. Immediately, it can feel like we succeeded, almost as if the lie itself felt better to accomplish than the assignment. Yet, if the pride in the lie exceeds the pride in the assignment, then either you, the teacher, or both have not succeeded in your communication and/or learning roles.

Unfortunately, some teachers may establish their curriculum to encourage pride in the lie over the assignment, which is typically a sign of something the teacher invited with their own negative approaches, such as bragging about how the class has a high-fail rate. It can make a student feel that it's safer to make a lie their go-to savior, in an attempt to create breathing room, than to ask the teacher for help.

There is another angle that students (and teachers) can forget: deception costs, while honesty rewards.

I know of one teacher, who had a student who said her grandmother was in the hospital. The professor showed compassion and wanted to know what hospital the grandmother was in so she could send flowers. The student had been one the that teacher regarded as upstanding. The professor wanted to be there for her good pupil in her time of struggle. Eventually, the student admitted to lying. The teacher then remembered that student and used her as an example in her lectures as the type of student she will never write a letter of recommendation for.

In comparison, I once messed up my final exam essay. I was leaving the university, thinking that I was done with my work and could go home to prepare for my last final exam the following day. I looked at my calendar and realized the final exam was actually due in one hour, not the next day. I ran to the testing center and scratched out the worst essay I'd ever written.

Later, I was speaking with my professor, and she told me that I blew the exam, and she asked what happened. She was a professor who instructed her students that "death is no excuse from the final." Naturally, many students were afraid of her. I told her what had happened, and she didn't allow the assignment to keep me from getting an A in the class. Her reasoning was that all semester, I had been the highest performing student. She'd also had me in two previous classes, and she knew what I could do, and that this was a hiccup. Because I was honest with her, she saw through that hiccup and felt she could justify the work based upon the record I had previously established with her.

Unlike my former professor who made me feel like I had to pretend a page was torn from my essay just to get a fair shake in his class, the more demanding teacher showed me a leniency that I did not expect. She allowed the honesty that I had accumulated with her to help her overlook my stupid mistake in nearly missing my final exam in her class. Because of that, somewhere in her brain, she told herself: "I feel comfortable rewarding this student with leniency."

The point is that a semester is fifteen weeks long. Although deception may buy you breathing room for a day or weekend to allow you to submit an assignment you didn't finish on time. It's the honesty that teachers remember that makes themselves more likely to support you in the long-run. It may take fifteen weeks to see the benefit of that honesty and genuine interaction, but it will show. When teachers interact with honest and genuine students, those professors are more likely to do everything in their power to sustain those students in their goals.

You don't typically see heated arguments from teachers regarding student grades unless there has been some level of deception or lack of interest from either the student or the teacher. If an honest student is at an A- in a class, and that student has a history of being honest, and puts up a minimal argument about if it's possible to raise that A- to an A, it's highly possible the teacher will offer options to raise the grade. I promise teachers have done that with students who have played honestly, for no other reason than that history of truthfulness.

Likewise, I promise that students who have lied and are trying to argue for that same grade bump, will get teachers who will not budge entirely based on the dishonesty. In those cases, you'll more likely find a teacher thinking, "Not a chance. In fact, if I could ignore the grading established in this class, I would knock you down a grade because of your dishonesty with me."

The rewards of honesty may be slower, but the support system far surpasses the dishonest immediacy.

One of the most effective ways to turn a teacher against ever wanting to go the extra mile for you, is to lie to them, and more importantly about them. Be above that, because honesty's an attitude that will give you an edge over the students who cause other teachers to say, "We won't believe what your students say about you, if you don't believe what your students say about us."

To bring it home. To date, I have never written a letter of recommendation for a student who lied to me or lied about me. And they have asked. There are some though that, if they asked, I would write them a letter, and that letter would open with: "This student has a history of lying to me. If you're looking for a dishonest candidate for a sales position, this person's really good at it."

Professors of the Soup Rules

Professor of the SOS or VICE W

Student Perspective:

Despite the illusion you've seen in college ads and posters, school will not always be a happy, joyous place where you're surrounded by smiling friends and have a lot of time to do all the fun, exciting things you want to do. College is hard. It is grueling, frustrating, time-consuming, and exhausting. On top of all of the hardships you'll have when it comes to living situation, food, homework, social life, and mental well-being, there are going to be times when you don't get along with your professors.

There! I said it. Not every class you take is going to be choice, and not every professor you have will be your favorite either. In my time at school, I had professors that I really enjoyed, and who went above and beyond their task as a teacher to help me succeed, not just in their class but in my major and in life. I had one professor that I put as a reference on a resume, and she helped me get my current job. I have one professor that still sends out emails to our class from years ago, just bringing up things he thinks we would be interested in. And, I have another professor who I'm writing a book with <Cough> Professor Fairchild <Cough>. These are the types of professors that you will get along with, enjoy, and will push you to be a better student and person.

Along with these extra-supportive professors, you'll get the type of teacher that will turn out to be about 80% of the professors you'll encounter as a student. You go to their classes, you do what's asked of you, you pass the class, and you move on. Sure, they might recognize you in the hall once or twice and give you a nice "hello," or maybe a "how are you doing," but not much more than that. In the same vein, you might think of their class or something they taught you once or twice in your lifetime. But, for the most part, you'll both drift by in each other's lives without much thought. And that is alright. That's how most of your experiences with professors will be like.

However, there will also be a few that, for some inexplicable reason, you do not get along with. Sometimes, this is because their class isn't a style that works well with you, or they talk too slow, or too fast, or they seem patronizing, or you just get a weird vibe from them. Most of these things will be out of your control. For some reason or another, some people are just not meant to get along. That is how the world works.

Although I said some of these things are out of your control, some of them are not. Before I get into the main point of this section, I want to let you know that if you, in anyway, think that a reason you don't get along with a professor is because of a core aspect of who you are such as race, religion, gender, physical appearances, disabilities, etc. then let someone over the department know. There will be times you don't get along with a professor, that is true, but it should never be because of something out of your control.

Now, back to my previous statement: There will be teachers you dislike without any fault of either of you, just a clash in personalities and teaching and learning styles. However, what you should not do is lie about it, whether to yourselves or others. Sometimes, we blame a professor for us not succeeding when we are the cause. That is an example of lying to ourselves. I've been there.

I had a really tough test, and I didn't do well. Any time I or anyone else brought it up, I would complain about the professor and their teaching style.

"They were the reason I failed, not the fact that I had spent my nights watching shows instead of studying. No. It was because that professor had it out for me, and their class was way too hard anyways! They're not a good teacher, so who can blame me?"

Now, that is not to say that teaching doesn't influence how well you do in a class. But unless nearly everyone else is failing the course too, I think you can confidently rule out the professor being the sole reason you didn't pass that exam. We often use this as a defense mechanism when we know we could have studied better and tried harder. It's so easy to cast the blame on someone else, but deep down you know that they aren't the reason you failed.

Along with using a professor as a scapegoat for your shortcomings, some students take to slandering a professor solely because they don't like them. More often than not, these can seem like harmless little sayings when you're around your friends.

However, what many students forget to do is humanize their professors. Your professor is (most likely) not some eldritch being that has a knowledge of all things and knows exactly how to keep you focused in class. In fact, as you'll soon figure out, your professors are (mostly) normal individuals who have a love of learning and a lot of knowledge on what they're teaching. So, even if you don't get along with them, remember, they're just human with similar struggles and frustrations as you. What may seem like a harmless lie about them can be extremely hurtful, not just to the professor but their career. So, you might not like someone. Get over it! College isn't going to be a breeze. So, adapt and work on yourself, not what you can't change.

Here, on the topic of lying, one of the worst things a student can do is not just lie about their professor but *to* their professor. Sometimes, you have a really good reason. You came in late to class and your professor warned you that coming in late one more time would affect your grade. However, your cousin Stacy called you and had to talk about how Brad broke up with her.

After listening to her, you knew you'd be late to class if you stopped and grabbed your morning Starbucks. You need your Starbucks. Of course, you had to get it. And then the line was too long. So, of course you were late to class.

Sometimes, you think, "Hey. No problem. I'll just tell Professor Lane that I was late because of a family emergency, and it will be fine."

Now let me tell you why this lying is a terrible idea. One, it's going to catch up with you eventually. You can only have so many family emergencies and struggles before someone will start asking questions. And two, taking advantage of your professor in this way betrays the trust that they have in you, and building trust with a professor is one of the best things you can do to succeed in college.

How so?

Well, when I was a junior in college and had started to get the hang of things more, I was doing pretty well in school. I was used to the whole horse-and-pony show, and I was able to get my assignments in on time with a high enough quality that this is soon what professors expected from me (because of the trust we had established). I would show up on time, if not a bit early. I would do my work, ask questions, and overall do exactly what was expected.

So, when actual emergencies or exceptions came along, how do you think my professors reacted?

They showed me leniency. They helped me get back on my feet if I was deathly ill, had a family emergency or even just really needed to miss class.

Why?

Because they knew I wouldn't lie to them, and that—when I really needed help—I needed it. So, establishing this trust and respect with a professor is far more beneficial to you, as a student, than lying. I'm not saying you need to be buddy-buddy with professors, and that they need to know all of your life's details. However, showing that you respect them and their classes will help ensure they give you that same respect in return and at a time when you need it most.

Not lying seems like a pretty good golden rule to have, but sometimes, things like harmless jokes or fast excuses can slip out. However, keeping honesty in your work and with your professor will help you maintain trust in your relationships with them. This is way more precious than getting out of a one-time thing or making yourself look good.

Take my advice and stay honest. I promise you that school will become that much easier.

Student

view

8 — Unfair Requests
reap what you sow

"Success in the United States is not an entitlement
in China. You have to go there and earn it,
and earn it the right way."

—Howard Schultz—
(Businessman/Author)

Professor Perspective:

I have a black marker. Here. I'll hold it high so everyone can see it. Now, watch me write on this whiteboard. Watch me write the word, *Marker*. See it? Yeah, I know. My handwriting is bad.

As a teacher, I have many tools. I have a tablet, a computer, a bag that can carry other tools, such as more markers and tic tacs (because I don't want to kill students with bad breath).

What's interesting about all of these tools is that not one of them, even though I have them, is what guarantees that I get to keep teaching classes. It's not a pass that I hand to my department head and say, "here's my black marker, give me my class roster."

I get to use the black marker to help me teach, because I've shown that I can teach. That is what allows me to keep teaching.

If I were to be a bad teacher, and you (the student) complained—and I didn't get fired because of it—you would find it unfair. You would be outraged if the department ignored

Professor (vertical, right margin)

your complaint and my bad work ethic and simply said, "We can't fire him. He has a black marker. If we fire him, his black marker might dry up." You'd find it unfair because you know that it takes more than a black marker with ink for a teacher to actually earn their station to lead a classroom.

However, if we flip this scenario to where the student is the recipient of such an unfair suggestion, then suddenly students tend to support it, and they don't realize the damage it causes to their own classmates and their university environment.

For instance, many people earn scholarships. These are contract-rewards between the grantor and the student that says if the students keep earning good scores, the grantor will keep paying for that student's education. However, I have had more students with scholarships try to guilt me into thinking that if I don't give them a higher grade than they earned in a class, that they'll lose the scholarship. Quite frankly, if this is the case, they should lose the scholarship because the student did not keep up their end of the contract.

Not once has a bank ever forgiven someone's mortgage and given away a free house to a borrower who said, "but if you don't give me credit for making payments even though I haven't, I could lose my home."

Suggesting that I, a professor, should be allowed to keep teaching because I have a black marker is no different than suggesting a student should be allowed a higher grade because they have a scholarship. If this is how a student values their scholarship, then that scholarship is worthless, and so is the degree that a student may have enticed teachers to grant grades towards.

It is an unfair request to ask a teacher to give you a reward based upon a trophy that you've already obtained. To date, no football team has ever been allowed into the Superbowl simply because that team may have won the Superbowl the previous year.

One of the biggest ways that students sabotage themselves in the classroom is believing that they have a right to high marks that they haven't earned simply because they've gotten good grades before.

I often get comments from students that sound like this, "I believe I should get an A in your class. I only missed six days and two major assignments." Then, I have to say, "So what should I give the person who didn't miss any classes and turned in all of their assignments? Because you clearly didn't even attempt to do the same work that the other student accomplished, and that student is getting an A. Do you really think you've earned the top grade that this class has to offer by not turning in work and not coming to class? Do you think you deserve the same grade as other students who have far surpassed what you've given?"

Then that student will quite often answer with a "yes" and then proceed to justify how they shouldn't be punished just because another student performed better throughout the semester. Let's be clear, no one gets punished because another student performs well or better than you. Students simply don't get rewards they haven't earned. It's not another student's fault that you didn't do your work or got the grade you earned on your own.

Other students have tried to guilt trip me into a reward that they did not earn with statements such as, "If I lose my scholarship, it will be your fault." To which, I respond with, "I'm not the one who broke your contract by not turning assignments in on time. You did that all on your own."

This kind of blaming-approach doesn't train you to excel as a student. It doesn't train you to be average. It trains you to make excuses and to be unreliable. This will follow you into your careers. What you practice in college, you take with you into the working world. Your employers, clients, co-workers, partners, etc. will learn you make excuses and cut corners, and those aren't the attitudes that get people invested in you.

Sure, it might entice a teacher somewhere to give you something you haven't earned, but that will only reinforce a student's habit to believe they deserve something they haven't worked to obtain.

This kind of habit will burn bridges with your professors, the very people who have contacts and influence to help you get into programs and possibly jobs.

One of the biggest disservices that students can do to themselves is to expect reward when you have not earned it.

Many students have been taught, and I've seen the teachers who have contributed to this myth, that points are something that are taken away from you as you work rather than something you earn. It's an approach of: "I start everyone out with full points, and the more mistakes you make, the more points I take off."

Because of this students often make inaccurate assumptions such as, "I got docked points" as if the student actually had points to begin with, which you didn't. You didn't enter class with 100% of your points and then have them subtracted as you progressed. You entered the class with zero points, and then you received them accordingly for doing what was asked of you.

So, reality check: You, a student, don't get something for doing nothing. You do stuff, the teacher pays you for it with points. Do it well, and you could get rewarded with a scholarship.

You'll never find an employer who'll say, "K, I'm going to pay you an entire year's wage up front, and every time that you don't do your job or don't show up for work, I'm going to bill you for a partial refund."

When you get into the realistic mindset that points are rewards, you will develop a better respect of what you actually have and have not done to earn those rewards. Maybe there was a time elementary teachers had to give every student a trophy to keep children from crying and parents from screaming, but this isn't elementary school. You're adults now. You don't get something for nothing. Just because you got rewarded for giving something in the past doesn't mean you get to start giving less in the present, and it's not the teacher's fault if you do that. Your teacher didn't do your work in these situations. Then again, if your work's missing, neither did you. It's unfair to expect teachers to reward you, as students, for what you didn't do.

This simple understanding helps a student see the difference between attitudes of "I showed up. What more do you want?" and "I can make this better!"

There is no docking points. Either you do the work and earn points, or you don't do the work and don't earn points.

*** Professors! Incoming bonus of how a teacher can sabotage students.***

Some teachers have done some serious harm to students and stirred anxiety in the classroom, by allowing pupils to believe that the reason they didn't get full points is because points were taken from them, not awarded to them. This creates a false sense of ownership among students over those points that students never had in the first place. And this causes them to make those statements of "I got docked points."

Put yourself in the students' shoes here. When you lose something that you perceive belonged to you (whether it really did or not), you feel robbed when you also perceive that someone took it from you. That makes you want it back. You will even fight for it. When the teacher suggests the student starts a semester with points that they never had, no wonder students fight so hard to get something that was never in their possession in the first place. This fuels "please-give-me-something-I-did-not-earn" attitudes.

If you're a teacher who has used a "I give you everything, but take it away after," then you've invited the kind of unfair requests students bring to you, because you're the one who gave students the illusion of owning something they never had. You don't rob them of points, because they never had them, but you do rob them of classroom reality. You created the unfair environment.

However, students, that still does not mean you shouldn't be aware of the consequences of unfairly requesting what you have not earned.

Unfair requests come when we don't respect the reward.

Failing to understand the principles of reward lead to unfair requests, unhappy time spent in school, and a future where you don't strive to earn.

Did I say "earn?"

I meant learn.

Professors view

Student Perspective:

Recently, I was watching a television show while I cooked dinner, and I came across an interesting episode that showed a type of stereotypical college student that we tend to see a lot in the media. In this show, the main character was an assistant teacher for a college professor while also teaching her own beginning English class for non-majors.

Because her class was at a lower level, she ended up with a lot of student athletes, namely a famous basketball student that was currently elevating the university with his athletic skill. This made the student incredibly cocky and lazy about his learning, and he didn't take it seriously. The main character did all she could to help him, even catering lesson plannings around him such as describing a book and the character's actions in sports terms, so he might have an easier time understanding it.

Despite all of this effort, and the sports star even seeming like he might enjoy class a little more, he was still not turning in assignments. When she tried to give him a failing grade for not turning in school work (despite giving him multiple chances), the student was flabbergasted. He claimed that she couldn't possibly do this to him, because if he failed this class, he would lose his scholarship and couldn't play on the team anymore. If he couldn't play on the team, it would lose without him. Then all the bad publicity on the school would be her fault.

Although this scenario was exceedingly dramatized, we see this type of student in media a lot. This is the student who thinks he can fly under the radar in his classes and get a grade just for showing up. They often develop the attitude of they deserve a good grade, or they need a good grade and thereby they should receive it. The reason this stereotype shows up so much in film, books, and other media is because they really do exist.

Now, unlike in film, these attitudes are not just found in student athletes. In fact, this type of student comes from anywhere, and can even be you if you're not careful. In my experience, this type of demanding student is formed from a single feeling: entitlement.

When you think of the word entitlement, you're probably imagining a middle-aged woman, who's probably named Karen, with a short blonde haircut and an ill-fitting blouse. Maybe you see her yelling at some poor minimum-wage worker and wants to speak to their manager. Although I think this is an excellent description of entitlement, it's not quite what an entitled student is. In my experience an entitled student usually comes in one of three different forms that we'll discuss: Sporty Sams, Intellectual Idas, and Lazy Liams.

The first that we briefly touched on at the beginning are the Sporty Sams. Now Sporty Sams aren't always the star of whatever team they're on, trying desperately to keep their sports scholarship and place on the team. No. Sporty Sams can also just be the students who think they're too busy with other things and should get a pass on certain assignments and classes because of it.

Sporty Sams don't necessarily have to be on a team at all. These students can be Yogi's, trail bikers, pickleball enthusiasts, or even just professional party people and thrill-seekers. The main trait is they're too busy doing other things to spend all their time in a classroom, or at home studying—and they make sure that everyone else knows that it's beneath them too.

These are the students who try to get an extension because they had too much going on, or they ask the professor if they can have some more bonus assignments because they couldn't bother to try hard enough on the original ones. If any of this sounds sneakingly familiar to you, I might have some bad news for you, you might be a Sporty Sam.

These students form a lot during freshman year because the university world is a new experience, and there's so much to try. No wonder you get a little overwhelmed and want a break.

Student View

However, all Sporty Sams end up coming to a rude awakening eventually. So, if Sporty Sam doesn't want to learn the hard way, he needs to start taking his classes a little more seriously and sacrificing fun, every once in a while, for the rewards of studying and learning. After all, that's the real reason you're at college, right?

On the other side of the spectrum from the Sporty Sams, we have the Intellectual Ida.

Where Sams don't take things seriously enough, Idas take things way *too* seriously. They're the first to turn things in and the last ones to leave the classroom. With a mindset like that you might be confused about how an Intellectual Ida could ever make an unfair request.

This comes in two different forms. The first is that sometimes Idas think that tasks or assignments are beneath them. Perhaps they feel that they've already mastered something, or that it's not worth their time or energy to focus on it—for instance, a high scoring math major who thinks the astronomy class they're forced to take is worthless, as well as the molecular biology student forced to take what they view as an unrelated poetry class.

Whatever type of Intellectual Ida they are, they find things unworthy of their level of skill and, thereby, try to get out of it by claiming the class is too easy. It's beneath them, but it's fine for everyone else, so Idas thinks they should be exempt.

Other forms of Intellectual Idas can become so wrapped up in their studies that they get burned out and overwhelmed and feel that they deserve special attention or exemptions because they're struggling. After all, they're usually extraordinary in class, so shouldn't they get a pass just this once?

As you might guess from these two examples, Idas were usually the teacher's pet in high school.

Although not necessarily a bad thing, Intellectual Idas can get it into their heads that they are just always meant to succeed. Then, when they encounter difficult obstacles, they think other people (especially professors) should bend over backwards for them. Unfortunately for them, that is not the case.

If you're an Intellectual Ida keep your thirst for knowledge, but don't let your academic prowess fool you into thinking you deserve extra things because of it. Try something new that you think might be beneath you, you might have fun. Also, never expect to get a pass just because you're trying hard. Plan your schedule well to avoid burnout and let yourself have a break every once in a while.

Last, but not least, are Lazy Liams. Lazy Liams appear often in the junior and senior years of college. These are the students who feel that it is no longer worth their effort to try and, instead, will do anything to get out of or to fudge an assignment. These are the people who take naps in boring classes, get on their phone during group projects and do their best to not attend a morning class.

Although burn out can create a Lazy Liam, oftentimes they're just born out of sloth and the desire to get away with not doing something. These are the students who ask for easier assignments, asking dumb questions (see chapter three), and more test help. They want to be given the answers, not to have to seek them themselves. They want to be given an A, but not have to earn it.

The entitlement really shines through on Lazy Liams because, more often than not, they don't have anything to hide it under. While Sporty Sams cling to their busy schedules and Intellectual Idas cling to their ability to try too hard, Lazy Liams just want to be given things.

Why?

Well, just because. So, how do you avoid being a Lazy Liam? Simple. You have to have a drive and motivation. Don't let yourself get caught up in how hard things are. Focus on what you're doing right, what you like to do, who you like to be with. Try to keep that good motivation going.

Now that we've discussed the three different types of entitled students, you're aware of what it means when one of them makes an unfair request. They want something they haven't earned. Obtaining this attitude—whether you're a

Student Vie W

Sporty Sam, Intellectual Ida, or Lazy Liam—is a dangerous slope to tread on, which will only lead to disappointment and anger.

Don't expect anything free in life, especially in college. The only way to succeed and to feel proud of doing so is to put forth your own effort. Trust me, most professors won't be giving you any handouts, and the ones that do won't be doing you any favors in the real world if they do.

Student view

9 — Effort
| *building jello freeways* |

"We are being ruined by the best efforts of people
who are doing the wrong thing."

—W. Edwards Deming—
(Composer, author, economist)

Professor Perspective:

First of all, if you skipped reading my introduction to this book, there's no sense reading on until you go back and read it, as that's precisely the reason we chose to write this book to help university students succeed. Especially for this chapter point.

Every semester, I get a handful of students who will be asked to accomplish a task such as write a particular type of essay that issues certain bits of information. Rather than turn in a finished product of the assignment, they turn in something entirely different. For instance, I might ask students to submit a research proposal, and they will give me an argument instead. Now, the researched argument may be brilliant, but it is not a research proposal, and that is what I have to evaluate at the time. I have to judge the assignment as a proposal not an argument. When a student hands me an argument instead of a proposal, it tells me that the student cannot write a proposal—so, I need to focus on helping that student better understand how to craft a proposal.

Obviously, the student is understanding, right?

Wrong. Many say, "But I worked hard on this. I put in a lot of effort!"

Ah! The Jello freeway spills again.

It's as if the word *effort* is supposed to act as some official excuse to give students a free pass in class not to learn how to do the assignment. I do believe effort (the wrong effort) should be an excuse, just not the way many students think. Instead of supporting the student, I think it should give a free pass to whatever string of swear words or reality check a professor wants to throw at the student.

"Why are you yelling at that student?"

"She said 'effort,'"

"Oh, well, if she said 'effort,' carry on."

Then I square a tuba right in the student's face and give her a good, old WAH-Wah-waaaaaaah!

As a professor, every time a student who exerts the wrong kind of energy and then throws the word *effort* out there as an argument for a higher score, I believe that their teacher should rub that student's face right into the word the same way so many ignorant dog owners rub their dogs' noses in poop to get them to stop doing their doodies on the rug. Except rubbing a student's nose into the misunderstanding of what effort means actually works.

How is this sabotage?

Employers want people who accomplish tasks. In a world where the norm is becoming that we should reward people who make excuses, employers still need to function properly, and they can't do that with employees going, "But I put in a lot of effort, why are you firing me?"

"Because you cost us billions of dollars building a Jello freeway, and I cannot afford to have employees around who cost me that kind of money."

When students say, "But I put in a lot of effort," they are training themselves to make excuses to perform tasks incorrectly, and no one who does that has a successful career with limitless potential.

As a professor, my job is not to grade if you worked hard. Everyone in your class works hard. Hell, I work hard trying not to tear up student's papers when I find myself yelling at them going, "We talked about this thirty-thousand freaking times. I looked right at you even when you asked, 'how do I?' And I even drew you pictures on how to do the task." However, my job is to judge whether you, the student, accomplished a task or not, and how effective the methods you used to accomplish that task were.

If you didn't accomplish the task, I'm not going to pretend that you did, especially when I have a room full of students who did.

Employers are more selective. If they have one person who works hard and accomplishes tasks given to them, they are not going to reward the person who doesn't. Likewise, if you go to that employer and say "but I work hard," that employer is going to say, "Better luck next time" until you finally get the effort right, or they fire you.

Universities are training grounds for you, as students, to enter society with an understanding of how to accomplish tasks, so that you don't have to be trained as much in the workforce and so you can hit the ground ready to lead. What kind of a leader or employee are you preparing yourself to become if you train yourself to make excuses with "but I worked hard?"

This is the very real response you're going to get in the workplace if you say this:

"Did you accomplish the job, or at least get closer to finishing it?"

"Well, no, but I worked hard."

"No one cares! Do the job, or you can look for another one."

That's not the only way that right effort or wrong effort can influence though. Your wrong effort can affect others.

For example, the worst student I ever encountered was Anne (not her real name). Anne shows up to class, and puts in great effort to show that she does not need to be there. When a teacher introduces a specific fact, rather than question in class (a place for questions), she turns to the person next to her and she says, "That's not true." At this point, the second student gets caught up in Anne's energy.

Not only does the person next to Anne hear her, but the entire class does, and the entire class grows tired of hearing it. The person next to her begins to also adopt the attitude that it is okay to call the professor a liar in his classroom rather than question his comments. Now, Anne and the student sitting next to her begin to infect a third student with their anti-classroom and anti-scholarly behavior.

Professor's

View

Soon, three people are muttering nonsense and upsetting the class. They stop listening. It gets so bad, they even begin to hear what was never said. They claim the teacher made statements in the class, which makes other students turn to them out of frustration and argue, "He never said that!"

Anne was so self-centered and oblivious to her own community that she actually thought she was putting in the right kind of effort and doing a good job. She was not. Her wrong kind of effort actually put other students' grades in jeopardy. Then she blamed the teacher for not rewarding her more.

The sad part about this story is that Anne never learned because she refused to. She was one of those students that I still look back on and know that, some day, she will be sitting at the same crappy job, or one like it, complaining about how her degree is useless—not because it is useless, but because she founded it in the wrong effort.

She worked wrong, and insisted it was right. She behaved poorly, and insisted it was in good fun. She sabotaged others, and enabled them to sabotage themselves. Then, she still thought she should earn an A. The reality is that through her wrong effort, she became toxic. Toxic people in the real world rarely inspire and barely lead. In the event they actually acquire some kind of a throne, they are destined to fall from it, and fall hard. Wrong kind of effort isn't just a school trade, it's a life trade.

I never had a student who I looked at and said, "she has no business being in a university because she doesn't grasp what it's about" until I met Anne. Unfortunately, I know she's destined to spend an entire life screaming, "I worked hard. I put in a lot of effort." I know, unless she makes a huge adjustment in learning attitude and willingness to identify right effort and wrong effort, that she is destined to wonder why she never gets opportunities, and why people don't trust her to work in groups.

Insist on building Jello freeways in school, and you only prepare yourself to build them in the real world.

The key to succeeding with effort is to know just what makes the right kind of effort and being willing to discover and exercise it.

Student Perspective:

This may sound kind of silly, but it's not always enough to put in effort into your studies. I'm sure you've heard, your whole life though, that all that you need to succeed is a dream and a little elbow grease. While that is an excellent start, there's no use trying to fix a broken wall if you have a rubber hammer. No, in order to go anywhere with your goal, you also have to be focusing on the right type of effort.

This may be tricky to wrap your head around because you might struggle to understand what the wrong type of effort is in order to know what the right kind of effort is. After all, if you're studying for a class, how can any type of effort be wrong?

Let me share with you a funny example in my life to highlight this point of what the wrong type of effort is from the eyes of a child. When I was about eleven or twelve years old, I loved to play *Smash Bros*. In two modes of the game, you could play two-player or a co-op version where you would race around various stages playing different characters and completing goals to further the story. In the co-op version, the first player was kind of the leader. If that player died, you both had to start over. If player number two died, player number one, however, could continue. Along with that, if player one got too far ahead, player two could press a button (the A Button), and they would zoom up alongside player one in a little glowing sphere that couldn't be hurt.

Because of these rules, it was important that the strongest player fill the player one spot. This way, if the weaker player fell behind, the weaker player could just press A to catch up or to get out of danger if they were scared.

One day, I was playing with my younger cousin who we'll call Bella. Bella was a couple years younger than I was, and she loved to spend time with me in playing this game. She lovingly liked to call it *The Button Game*. Why? Because Bella got very good at pressing the A button at the right time to hide away in her little glowing ball.

The reason I share this is because Bella put in a lot of effort. If she didn't press the button at the right time to save herself, her

S
t
u
d
e
n
t

V
i
e
w

game character could die, get hurt, or get left behind. However, instead of learning how to catch up to me, how to fight back, or how to get out of tricky situations, she instead put effort into learning the perfect time to push the button.

It was certainly an effort, but it wasn't the right type of effort. Meanwhile I was sitting there, struggling to keep our team alive and hacking at enemies when she just appeared when it was convenient. She never really fought at all, which was the whole point of the game and made it a lot more difficult on me as player one.

Don't worry. I wasn't frustrated at Bella for playing the game wrong, because technically that is a correct way to play the game. I was just frustrated that she wasn't putting her focus into the other aspects of what we were supposed to do, making it harder on me and her to play.

This is the same as the classroom. Too often, as students, we put effort into our assignments, but it's the wrong kind of effort. An example of this would be trying to memorize all of the answers to a test instead of actually trying to understand the material. Another would be trying to write a paper you think your professor will enjoy instead of one you actually believe in and want to argue. Then there's writing the famously bad essay and figuring out how to do things with the least amount of effort, instead of just figuring out how to do it right.

This is what I mean by the wrong type of effort. Instead of focusing on how to do their task correctly, oftentimes, students focus on how to do their work in the easiest, most fun, or unique way. It may seem that you're going the full mile to do your work. In actuality though, you may be taking a shortcut with the wrong tools and building a Jello freeway.

An example of this type of work in a student setting actually happened when I was in Professor Fairchild's class. One of our first assignments, before we figured out his teaching and our own learning style, came in the form of crafting an annotated bibliography. He gave us an example and then sent us on our merry way with strong warning to really look at the instructions and the example. Now, as a student, and even just a human being, I am a huge worrywart, and Professor Fairchild's class just amplified that in me. So, I spent hours perfecting my annotated bibliography, looking at his example (which was in APA not MLA, which most humanities students are used to), and I even got help and advice from an older student.

When I got to class on the day it was due, I found that most of the students had put a different type of effort into this assignment. They had focused more on the context of the annotation, or they had thought they found out how to do it easier with generators like EasyBib. And they failed the assignment.

Plenty of people put in work, but it ended up being the wrong type of effort as the class quickly found out. They had spent their time trying to figure out how to complete the assignment fast instead of how to complete it right. After we got our grades back, that stayed an example to me of where to focus my efforts when it came to assignments and what rewards I would reap with that attitude.

I don't share this story to say that this is the way you must do things in order to succeed, but rather to help you realize where to put forth your efforts. I'm sure I didn't need to do all the things that my over analyzing brain made me do to prepare the assignment, but I was focused on doing the project right instead of just completing it.

The point of the metaphor of the Jello Freeway is that you're given the tools to succeed, you're given the maps and the goal in mind but what falls on you is using the right materials and concentrating your efforts into completing it correctly.

So, when you're given a tricky new assignment, test, essay, or other project, the first step is to look at the tools you've been given. What can you work with? Do you have books at your disposal? Or is it a group assignment where you can get help from peers? Or can you maybe use the internet? After realizing what tools you have, take a look at your map. What are you expected to build or complete? Does your professor have an example of that *perfect* freeway? Better yet, do they have tips and tricks on how to complete it? Next, see what your own personal flair can do to help the assignment.

Work shouldn't be boring when you're putting in the right effort, but rather putting in the right effort should give you the freedom to put your own spin on it. When you do these things and focus on what you want to accomplish and go about building it the right way, I promise you that your freeway will be something that you can actually drive on and not just a delicious sugary treat.

S
t
u
d
e
n
t

V
i
e
W

10 — Burnout

| *taking on too much* |

P
r
o
f
e
s
s
o
r

V
i
e
w

"To err is human, but when the eraser wears out ahead of the pencil, you're overdoing it."

—Josh Jenkins—
(Australian Rules Football Player)

Professor Perspective:

Four years is a long time to work towards a bachelor's degree. It takes time, energy, lots of effort (especially the right kind). You do not get that diploma without this kind of sacrifice. There are days when you will feel down-trodden and absolutely beaten. You will have teachers you don't think listen, teachers who don't cater to you, teachers who scare you. But you will have teachers that you treat badly too and don't realize it.

We have many obstacles as students. I had them myself.

In my experiences, despite the obstacles that an individual may encounter, there are really three myths that contribute to overwhelming students. If you can learn how to deal with these myths, you can lighten the stress you encounter in your studies.

These myths are:

1. I must graduate in four years.
2. I must take every class I've signed up for, especially if I attended the first day already."
3. I must pass or withdraw (failing is the end of the world; and never audit).

You're going to be given a lot of counsel when it comes to your university life. Some of that will deal with your workload. It can be overwhelming counsel. It can be counsel that makes you feel like you've lost hope. That's a horrible place for any student to be.

There's one piece of counsel that mentors and advisers don't give students enough though:

It's okay to lighten your load!

I'm not saying that being a full-time student doesn't work, nor that it should be abandoned. I'm saying, if you're feeling overloaded, and you need to breathe or to work on your mental health, there is nothing wrong with knowing how to lighten your burden. Taking on too much can affect your mental and physical well-being.

For example, I don't know where this came from, but advisers will frighten students into thinking they have to take more classes than they need to be a full-time student. They'll make potential students think they have to enroll right now. I had a recruitment adviser in grad school try to frighten me into starting sooner than I was ready. She made it seem that it would be the end of the world if I didn't start graduate school right when I was speaking to her.

My least favorite tactic I've seen is how many advisers make students think they must take 15 credit-hours per semester to be considered full-time.

No.

Twelve hours per semester is considered full time. That might not seem like much, but to a student who is feeling burdened down, that extra class can provide the breathing room a student needs to stay on top of their own health. Dropping a class to go from a 15-credit-hour load to 12-credit-hour load, may just be what the student needs to lower their anxiety levels.

There is nothing wrong with lightening your load. Adding value to who you are is not a race against time to get that degree. Additionally, if being a full-time student is too much, there is nothing wrong with being a part-time student.

I've seen many students destroy themselves in school, lose hope, fall out of sorts, and turn to quick and unhealthy escapes all because they felt they had to do more (and faster) than they were physically and mentally capable of.

It's easy to take on too much, but it's not required.

Students will often blame teachers for the workload of a class that is typical of a course load, but they won't accept personal responsibility for taking on more work than they could handle.

When you feel you're going to be heading into a semester where you don't have a lot of time, and you see a syllabus on the first day of class that says, "We'll be writing fifty essays in this class." You can always look for a different teacher who might only have two essays. You could tell yourself, "Not this semester. Let's do this next semester, and I'll take something a little less demanding on me this semester."

If you're failing a class, it's easy to feel that you have no where to go but down. Yet, other than sting to personal ego, there's nothing wrong with taking the class again.

As students, we can get so caught up with the issue of graduating in a given time that we don't stop to remember learning is about us. We are the degrees. That piece of paper you receive from graduating is called a diploma. It's just a protocol to prove you were present while you were developing as the degree. Make no mistake though. *You* are the degree. What good are you going to be as a degree if everything about it has weighed you down until you have no more mental or physical strength to carry on into the professional world? In the field of nursing, for instance, a new term has emerged in dominance—nursing burnout. This is where students studying to become nurses are entering the workforce already burned out from school.

Students are often convinced that they have to take on too much. They often hear and believe advice such as: "You have to take this many classes if you want to graduate in four years"; "You have to take all these classes right now if you want to get into them"; "You need to get your general ed requirements out of the way as quickly as possible." Although it is all helpful advice, it is not always accurate, nor in the best interest of your overall well-being.

As an undergraduate student, I was given the latter piece of advice. Everyone said, "Get your gen eds done first."

I realized quickly that this piece of advice was killing my friends and peers off in their own studies.

I graduated with two bachelor degrees in four years, and I attribute the ability to do that by ignoring the advice to knock out gen eds early. In one of my degrees, there were higher-division classes I needed that came up every other spring. Some only came around in the fall. I would plan my calendar around those classes. I would fill in the blanks with gen eds to provide me the elasticity I needed to fill any gaps that might otherwise prevent me from maintaining full-time status. Sometimes, I took heavy workloads. Sometimes, I planned lighter semester loads. Sometimes, I attended school year-round. My last year of undergraduate work, I took my final general ed.

Despite what many students so often and mistakenly think, general eds and lower division does not mean easy. In fact, the historically most difficult college course has always been a general ed, lower-division class. So, there's a bit of stress to be had in taking all these high-stress, high-anxiety classes together just for the sake of knocking them out faster. Sometimes, mixing difficult classes (which you might not care about) with less demanding classes (which you might care about) can make a semester workload feel more bearable on your overall health.

As a student, I would watch peers working for a bachelor's degree kill themselves off trying to get their gen eds done so they could get their associate's degree in the process, and I would ask, "why? In two more years, you're just going to have your bachelor's and no one's even going to care you had an associate's." If all you're working on in is an associate's degree, sure you have to rip through your general eds, but if you're planning on working straight through to a bachelor's, it can be easy to let yourself get overwhelmed by feeling you need to also fulfill the requirements to earn your associate's degree along the way.

No. You don't have to. It might work into someone else's plan. That doesn't mean it has to be your plan. It wasn't in my plan.

Of all the degrees I have, none of them are associate's degrees. I'm not putting down associate's degrees. It's just that I, like many students, had the plan to work straight to a bachelor's degree. I identified that aiming for the associate's degree first was only going to make me feel that I had to do more than I really needed to get to that bachelor's. As long as I put in the time, it wasn't prudent for me to get an associate's in order to earn my bachelor's. So, I didn't get a two-year degree along the way. This tactic, I know, gave me more room to juggle my schedules so that I could balance difficult classes with less demanding ones.

Another tactic I did was I signed up for a minimum of 15 credit hours. One semester I had 21. If I felt I could accomplish the workload, I kept going. If not, I dropped classes.

I'm going to tell you a little secret. No one in the world cares whether you withdrew from a class or not. I know your advisers often scare you into thinking it matters. It does not. No one cares! It doesn't affect your GPA. It doesn't affect your academic standing. All it does is says that you were in the class and then you withdrew. If you have a W on your transcript, no one cares—not employers, not the university, no one (except maybe the occasional adviser trying to scare you).

Now, if you get an unofficial withdrawal (a UW), that's a different story. That affects everything related to university standing and even the ability to get financial aid. However, if you just choose to drop a class on your own accord and follow the appropriate steps to notify the university, NO ONE CARES!

What that means is that it's okay to drop a class. If dropping a class is what it takes to lighten your load, no one cares. The worst it's going to do is cause you to have to take a little longer to graduate. So what if it does? So what if it takes four-and-a-half or five years instead of four? It's better to feel sane at the end of five years than psychotically burned out at the end of four.

If taking 15 credit hours in the fall and spring becomes too much, you can try taking 12 in the fall, 12 in the spring, and consider six during the summer instead.

It's okay to look at a workload in a syllabus and say, "I'm not ready for a chemistry class alongside my composition class and my astronomy class. I'm dropping Chemistry, and I'll take it, and only it, in the summer."

To go with this, and this is one that a lot of people gasp over, it's okay to fail a class and take it again. It's okay to keep failing the class and taking it over and over. Heck, it's okay to get a high grade in a class and take it again just to get an even higher grade (lots of students do this to increase grad school acceptance chances). Sure, it might take you longer to master a topic of one class than it does others, but if you're willing to keep tackling the topic to master it, that's nothing to be ashamed of. I know that many students have been raised to feel ashamed of getting Fs in classes. An F in a class is nothing to be ashamed of unless you're going to use that F as a reason to give up. We learn the most about success through failure.

Anyone who tells you otherwise is dead wrong.

If you see that you're not going to pass a course, you can always try to change your enrollment to audit, which is a system the university specifically puts into place to allow people to attend and practice taking the class before they actually take it for a grade. There is no pass/fail or grade in an audit. You simply sit in on it and learn and prepare for all but the last few weeks of it.

Think of how much of a burden that could remove from a student who planned ahead to say, "I'm not doing well. My mental health is not in a good place. I'm going to explore my options of withdrawing or changing my status in the class to audit, and I'll retake the class at a better time for me."

If more students would take advantage of audit, there'd be less stress in the classroom. If more students would take advantage of dropping a class, there'd be fewer students burning out.

Students have become so trained to believe that school has an expiration date of four years on it, and this is simply not true. I've watched part-time students take eight years to graduate, and they were happier than any full-time student I've encountered (despite the part-time students also having a full-time job). I've seen students take ten years to earn a degree.

I've known employers who have given promotions that required degrees to employees without degrees simply because their employee was working on earning a degree. What's more, a few of the employers paid the students' tuition.

Not only did lightening their own loads help these students succeed and find a morale-boost in their full-time workplaces. These students also didn't have to add to their stress of worrying about paying back their student loans after they graduated.

I'm not saying that happens for everyone. I'm saying that there is no four-year expiration date to earn a degree. The degree doesn't turn into a pumpkin when the bell tolls midnight on the fourth year. However, there is not shortage of medical journals filled with research and doctor testimonials that stress does contribute to earlier expiration dates on a human life.

You don't have to kill yourself off getting a degree. You can lighten your load.

There is nothing wrong with being happy and taking fewer classes during your studies. One of the worst habits any student can do to harm their success in their learning is to simply insist on doing more than they should.

On a final note, as a teacher, I have had many students come in to a class after a point of no return (a time, we teachers know they can't recuperate a passing grade from). I've had many of these students tell me, "I'm going to prove you wrong. I'm going to prove that I can be the one to pass under these horrid conditions."

In fifteen years of seeing this in one particular class I've taught, I've seen only one student succeed in this attitude. The singular reason that she pulled it of was because it was the only class she decided to take and focus on. I'll tell you, she almost didn't make it. Every other student who thought they could come back from a point of no return, dropped, failed, or just plain disappeared from the classroom.

In addition to understanding that it's okay to lighten your load, know that it's okay to not have to insist on performing a near impossible belief of "I can do it" when a more helpful attitude might be, "I can do it, but maybe not right now. Maybe I should listen to the teacher who knows the class better than me when he suggests, 'I wouldn't recommend it.'"

Believe it or not, it's okay for students to breathe and do school on their own terms.

Student Perspective:

Alright, so throughout this book we've talked about ways that students can make college life difficult for themselves. Most of these have been tactics to get away with doing the bare minimum such as not reading the syllabus, taking lame notes, and asking for freebies. Despite all of this, I have found that one of the ways students most fail themselves in college is doing the exact opposite of trying too little. Instead, time and again, I see students take on too much, which inevitably leads to burnout and failure.

What exactly is burnout? We hear that term so often these days, but what exactly does it mean when you apply it to students? Now, the thing about burnout is it usually affects the students with the most ambition and the most drive which is what makes it so devastating. One of the key things I've seen is when students who did really well in high school end up doing average or less than in college. This can lead to a lot of self doubt, anger, depression and eventually burnout.

How do you avoid that?

This may seem cruel and perhaps a little mean, but the one thing that got me through college (as a prior excellent student in high school) was repeating to myself that I was just average. That's right, some people have moments in the mirror in the morning where they go, "You are amazing, you are special, and you can do it!" For me it was more like this: "You are just average. And that's okay! You are going to do your best though. You don't have to get the best grade in the class but you're going to get a good grade. You're not going to be the best, but you are going to be good."

You may be reading this and be absolutely horrified that this was my motivator, but, let me tell you, the first time I bombed a test, this was really comforting to me. I didn't have these lofty goals that I had no way to achieve. I was honest with myself. I had good, reachable objectives, and I liked myself and who I was. I knew that I could always try again and understood that one defeat didn't make me, as a person, a failure. Burn out comes from pushing too much on yourself and not being able to achieve it, so be kind to yourself! Accept that you won't be the best at everything (unless you are one of those crazy genius Einstein kids—in which case, what are you doing wasting your time listening to me?), and you'll be happier.

Another thing that leads to burnout is not being kind to yourself and your time.

So, let's talk about your first semester at school. For me I tried to stack on as much as I could. After all, I had scholarship requirements to meet, and on top of that I needed a way to pay for my housing needs along with monthly expenses. Because of this, I needed at least 16-credit hours and a part time job. Many of you are much the same. Some of you won't be working through school, some of you will. Some of you may need or may be required to take more or less credit hours, depending on your major and your schedule. No matter what the amount is, one of the key ways to avoid burnout is giving yourself some much needed personal time and rest from school.

Now, I don't mean a trip to Vegas every weekend. No. When I'm talking about breaks, I'm meaning something much simpler than that. One of the hardest semesters of my life was taking 18 credits. On Monday, Wednesday and Friday I was on campus from 8 a.m. to 8 p.m. without fail and with miniscule breaks in between. I was able to snag an hour between some classes to study or grab something to eat. You may ask, how did I survive without burnout? Trust me, I got really close to succumbing. However, Tuesdays and Thursdays I had no classes at all, which meant I could use that time to work. Luckily for me, my job was very therapeutic. I cleaned houses, which meant I could put in my music and scrub away while giving my mind some much needed time to reset.

Despite not seeming like a very relaxing time at all, I knew to grab my breaks when I could. That is one of the key parts of being a starving, exhausted student. You have to take the silent moments when you can. This means taking advantage of a few extra minutes before and after class to detox. It means being nice to yourself if you need a break from studying to maybe go for a walk.

Another fatal mistake students make that leads them straight to burn out is not asking for help when they are getting overwhelmed. I admit I am guilty of this. I'm the type of person that wants to do everything by herself. I want to be totally self-sufficient with my job, school, and personal life. But that's not how college works.

You will need help. Whether that be with certain classes, certain assignments, etc. there will just be things you quite simply won't be able to do without some form of help.

As I've repeated in previous chapters, do not be afraid to use your resources for help. I'm going to be beating a dead horse, but office hours are there for a reason. It is one-on-one time for you to go over something that is hard for you with the one person in your class who knows it the best: the Professor. There will also usually be study groups either with a TA or other classmates available. You don't have to do it alone.

One of the last but most vital ways to avoid burnout is to know when you have too much. This is one of the practices that people seem to forget or look over most of all, because— again—it goes back to pride, that concept of wanting to be able to do everything with no help. No one wants to appear weak, but, let me tell you, one of the strongest things you can do is to get rid of something extra because you know you can't handle it.

For example: My very last semester of school I wasn't aware it was going to be my last semester. Why? Because I was all signed up for classes and I was still missing an internship and one other class requirement in order to graduate. So, I figured I would have one more semester and then graduate. However, that's when everything fell apart, or rather started to come together. I went to the teacher of that last required class that I needed and asked the professor if he had any open slots. He said that he didn't but admired my drive, so he'd let me join anyways.

I then got an email that day telling me I had been accepted for the internship that I wanted.

I was baffled. Everything had fallen into place, except now I would be extremely busy. I had to give up my current job because the hours wouldn't coincide, and I had to resign from a head-position for a club that I had been ecstatic about. Still, I knew myself and I knew what I could and couldn't handle, and that meant dropping added stressors.

So, when you're in a class that very first day of school, and you're hearing the professor talk about all of the lab hours needed; the forty-three books you're required to read; the entire species of beetle you're required to save; and how many politicians you have to convince to tell the truth in order to pass the class, let me tell you this: It is okay to drop a class. You are not giving up or admitting defeat. You're putting a pin in it or going a different route. Don't wear yourself out to the point where you have no more willpower to do any more simply because you didn't want to seem like a quitter. Trust yourself, your schedule, and your ability, and you'll be on the right track. I can promise you that.

Student
Voice
W

Thank you for reading
Jello Freeways:
10 Ways Students Sabotage Their Efforts.

(Campus Nightmares Vol. 1)

We hope you found the information
in this book helpful.

Please share your experience by telling
a friend and leaving a review on your
favorite book review site.

For more on how teachers can sabotage
their students' studies, please check out:

Steering Classes off Cliffs:
10 Ways Professors Sabotage Students to
Crash and Burn

(Campus Nightmares Vol. 2)

www.ingramcontent.com/pod-product-compliance
Lightning Source LLC
LaVergne TN
LVHW051250080426
835513LV00016B/1838